Microsoft® Project 2013: Part 2

Microsoft® Project 2013: Part 2

Part Number: 091111
Course Edition: 2.0

Acknowledgements

PROJECT TEAM

Author	Media Designer	Content Editor
John Clinton Bradley	Alex Tong	Joe McElveney

Notices

DISCLAIMER

TRADEMARK NOTICES

Microsoft® Project 2013: Part 2

About This Course

Welcome to *Microsoft® Project 2013: Part 2*. This course is designed to familiarize you with the advanced features and functions of Microsoft Project Professional 2013 so that you can use it effectively and efficiently in a real-world environment.

In *Microsoft® Project 2013: Part 1,* you learned the basic features of Microsoft® Project Professional 2013 during the planning phase of a project. You gained the knowledge and skills to:

*   Create a new project plan. This includes starting a blank project file or starting a project file from a template.
*   Manage time in a project plan. This includes changing the project time frame and calendar.
*   Manage tasks in a project plan. This includes adding tasks and linking them together into paths.
*   Manage resources in a project plan. This includes adding people, equipment, and materials to a project and assigning them to tasks.
*   Share a project plan. This includes saving, printing, emailing, and exporting project files.

Microsoft® Project 2013: Part 2 covers the advanced knowledge and skills a project manager needs to update a project plan in Project 2013 during the execution, monitoring, and controlling phases of a project. In other words, once your project plan is approved by the project sponsor, this course will enable you to manage the project so that it is completed on time, within budget, and according to scope.

Each lesson in this course is built around the executing, monitoring, and controlling tasks that can be accomplished using the advanced commands found on one of these Project 2013 tabs: **PROJECT, TASK, VIEW,** or **REPORT.** This will enable you to become a "power user" and leverage the full potential of the application.

You can also use this course to prepare for the Microsoft Certified Technology Specialist (MCTS) in Microsoft Office Project 2013 certification.

Course Description

Target Student

Students taking this course are responsible for managing projects in a work environment. This includes creating and maintaining project plans.

Course Prerequisites

To ensure your success in this course, you should be able to create a new project plan, manage time in a project plan, manage tasks in a project plan, manage resources in a project plan, and share a project plan. This can be accomplished by taking the following Logical Operations course: *Microsoft® Project 2013: Part 1.*

Course Objectives

Upon successful completion of this course, students will be able to engage in advanced management of a project plan using Microsoft Project 2013.

You will:

- Manage the project environment.
- Manage task structures.
- Generate project views to manage a project.
- Produce project reports to share a project's status.

The LogicalCHOICE Home Screen

The LogicalCHOICE Home screen is your entry point to the LogicalCHOICE learning experience, of which this course manual is only one part. Visit the LogicalCHOICE Course screen both during and after class to make use of the world of support and instructional resources that make up the LogicalCHOICE experience.

http://www.lo-choice.com

Log-on and access information for your LogicalCHOICE environment will be provided with your class experience. On the LogicalCHOICE Home screen, you can access the LogicalCHOICE Course screens for your specific courses.

Each LogicalCHOICE Course screen will give you access to the following resources:

- eBook: an interactive electronic version of the printed book for your course.
- LearnTOs: brief animated components that enhance and extend the classroom learning experience.

Depending on the nature of your course and the choices of your learning provider, the LogicalCHOICE Course screen may also include access to elements such as:

- The interactive eBook.
- Social media resources that enable you to collaborate with others in the learning community using professional communications sites such as LinkedIn or microblogging tools such as Twitter.
- Checklists with useful post-class reference information.
- Any course files you will download.
- The course assessment.
- Notices from the LogicalCHOICE administrator.
- Virtual labs, for remote access to the technical environment for your course.
- Your personal whiteboard for sketches and notes.
- Newsletters and other communications from your learning provider.
- Mentoring services.
- A link to the website of your training provider.
- The LogicalCHOICE store.

Visit your LogicalCHOICE Home screen often to connect, communicate, and extend your learning experience!

How to Use This Book

As You Learn

This book is divided into lessons and topics, covering a subject or a set of related subjects. In most cases, lessons are arranged in order of increasing proficiency.

The results-oriented topics include relevant and supporting information you need to master the content. Each topic has various types of activities designed to enable you to practice the guidelines and procedures as well as to solidify your understanding of the informational material presented in the course. Procedures and guidelines are presented in a concise fashion along with activities and discussions. Information is provided for reference and reflection in such a way as to facilitate understanding and practice.

Data files for various activities as well as other supporting files for the course are available by download from the LogicalCHOICE Course screen. In addition to sample data for the course exercises, the course files may contain media components to enhance your learning and additional reference materials for use both during and after the course.

At the back of the book, you will find a glossary of the definitions of the terms and concepts used throughout the course. You will also find an index to assist in locating information within the instructional components of the book.

As You Review

Any method of instruction is only as effective as the time and effort you, the student, are willing to invest in it. In addition, some of the information that you learn in class may not be important to you immediately, but it may become important later. For this reason, we encourage you to spend some time reviewing the content of the course after your time in the classroom.

As a Reference

The organization and layout of this book make it an easy-to-use resource for future reference. Taking advantage of the glossary, index, and table of contents, you can use this book as a first source of definitions, background information, and summaries.

Course Icons

Watch throughout the material for these visual cues:

Icon	Description
	A **Note** provides additional information, guidance, or hints about a topic or task.
	A **Caution** helps make you aware of places where you need to be particularly careful with your actions, settings, or decisions so that you can be sure to get the desired results of an activity or task.
	LearnTO notes show you where an associated LearnTO is particularly relevant to the content. Access LearnTOs from your LogicalCHOICE Course screen.
	Checklists provide job aids you can use after class as a reference to performing skills back on the job. Access checklists from your LogicalCHOICE Course screen.
	Social notes remind you to check your LogicalCHOICE Course screen for opportunities to interact with the LogicalCHOICE community using social media.
	Notes Pages are intentionally left blank for you to write on.

1 Managing the Project Environment

Lesson Time: 1 hour, 50 minutes

Lesson Objectives

In this lesson, you will manage the project environment. You will:

- Link one project to another.
- Apply a project baseline.
- Add custom fields to a project.
- Change project options on the Backstage.
- Acquire Project 2013 apps from the Office Store.

Lesson Introduction

The commands on the **PROJECT** tab enable you to administer the project environment as a whole. In *Microsoft® Project 2013: Part 1* you learned how to use two tools on the **PROJECT** tab of the ribbon—the **Project Information** and **Change Working Time** dialog boxes—during the planning phase of a project. This lesson discusses several other tools on the **PROJECT** tab that you can use to manage a project during execution. It also discusses some of the other project options you can change on the **Backstage** and how you can extend Microsoft® Project 2013 with apps.

TOPIC A

Link Projects

Sometimes a project is completely independent from any other projects that may be occurring in the organization. Often, however, a project is connected to others. In this topic, you'll explore how projects link to one another and how to manage those connections.

Linked Projects

In *Microsoft® Project 2013: Part 1,* you learned how to link tasks within a project file. It is also possible to link separate project files, and to link tasks that are in separate project files. Linking projects, and tasks in different projects, establishes a relationship between the project files.

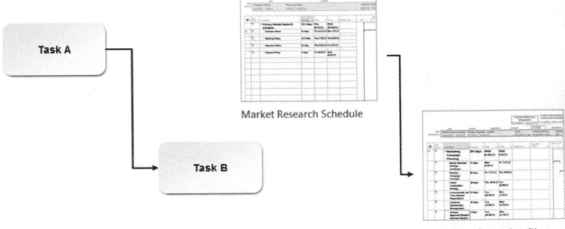

Figure 1–1: Linked tasks and linked projects.

Master Projects and Subprojects

A *master project* is one that is linked to one or more smaller subprojects. Conversely, a *subproject* is one that is linked to a larger master project. If you are managing a large, complex project, you may find it easier to create several small Project 2013 files and combine them with a master Project 2013 file. For example, the master project **Mission to Mars.mpp** might be composed of these subprojects:

- **Launch from Earth.mpp**
- **Travel from Earth to Mars.mpp**
- **Land on Mars.mpp**
- **Explore Mars.mpp**
- **Launch from Mars.mpp**
- **Travel from Mars to Earth.mpp**
- **Land on Earth.mpp**

One of the advantages to combining your subprojects into a master project is that it enables you to view all of your resources across projects and make sure none of them are overallocated.

You can easily link a subproject to a master project by selecting the **PROJECT** tab on the ribbon, finding the **Insert** command group, and selecting the **Insert Subproject** button.

Figure 1-2: Insert Subproject button.

> **Note:** To insert a subproject into a master project, you must be in a task-related view (such as **Gantt Chart** or **Network Diagram**). The **Insert Subproject** button will be disabled if you are in another type of view (such as **Calendar** or **Resource Sheet**).

> **Note:** To see summary data for a master project, unhide the **Project Summary Task**. In **Gantt Chart** view, select the **FORMAT** contextual tab on the ribbon, find the **Show/Hide** group, and check the **Project Summary Task** check box.

Insert Subproject Options

When you select the **Insert Subproject** button, the **Insert Project** dialog box will open.

Figure 1-3: Insert Project dialog box.

The **Insert Project** dialog box allows you three options for creating a link between the two files.

Option	Result
Link to project + Insert	A two-way link is established between the subproject and the master project. A change made in either file will be reflected in the other. This is the default option.
Link to project + Insert Read-Only	A one-way link is established between the subproject and the master project. A change made in the subproject file will be reflected in the master project file, but changes in the master file will not be reflected in the subproject file. This option protects the original subproject files from unwanted changes.
Insert	This option inserts a copy of the subproject data into the master project file. No link is established between the two files. A change made to either file will not be reflected in the other.

A subproject inserted into a master project looks and behaves much like a *summary task* (which you learned about in *Microsoft® Project 2013: Part 1*). You can expand the subproject in the master project to see the subproject's tasks. You can collapse the subproject in the master project to hide the subproject's tasks.

> **Note:** If you have a subproject with a two-way link to a master project, you can make a change to the subproject within the master project, and then save the master project. Project 2013 will ask you whether or not you want save the change to the subproject.

Dependencies

As you may recall from *Microsoft® Project 2013: Part 1,* when you *link* two tasks together in Microsoft Project 2013, you are creating a *dependency* between their start and finish dates. Dependencies drive the project schedule. A task may be linked to *predecessors* or *successors* . Every change you make to a linked task will affect its successors.

Types of Dependencies

This table shows the four types of dependencies that can exist between tasks.

Dependency	Description	Example
Finish-to-Start (*FS*) 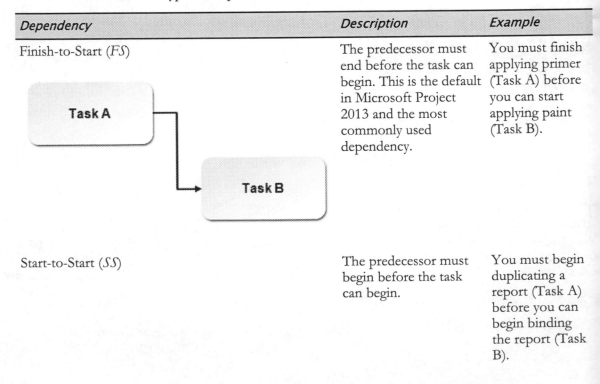	The predecessor must end before the task can begin. This is the default in Microsoft Project 2013 and the most commonly used dependency.	You must finish applying primer (Task A) before you can start applying paint (Task B).
Start-to-Start (*SS*)	The predecessor must begin before the task can begin.	You must begin duplicating a report (Task A) before you can begin binding the report (Task B).

Dependency	Description	Example

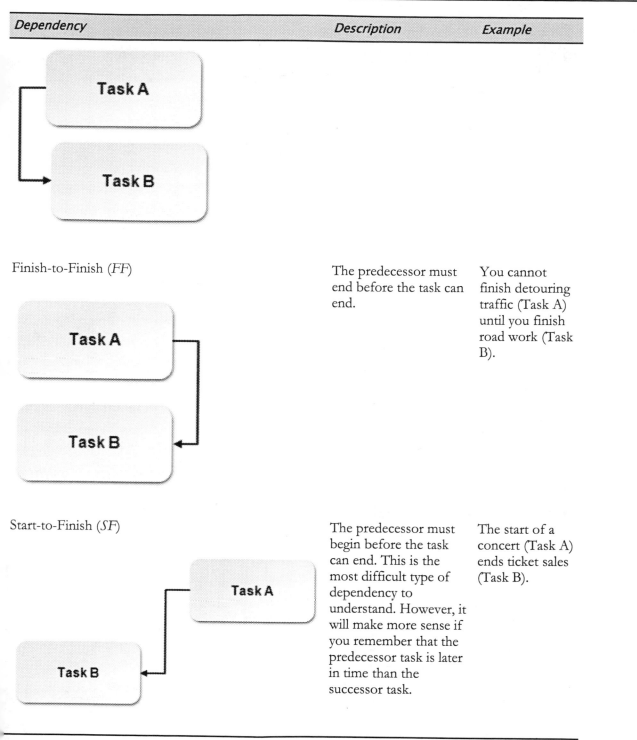

Finish-to-Finish (*FF*)

The predecessor must end before the task can end.

You cannot finish detouring traffic (Task A) until you finish road work (Task B).

Start-to-Finish (*SF*)

The predecessor must begin before the task can end. This is the most difficult type of dependency to understand. However, it will make more sense if you remember that the predecessor task is later in time than the successor task.

The start of a concert (Task A) ends ticket sales (Task B).

Task Links Between Projects

When subprojects are linked to a master project, you can establish dependencies between the tasks of the subprojects or between the tasks of the master project and its subprojects. This is done exactly like establishing dependencies between tasks in an independent project.

External Predecessors and Successors

You can easily see the dependences that exist between a project and other projects by selecting the **PROJECT** tab on the ribbon, finding the **Properties** command group, and selecting the **Links Between Projects** button.

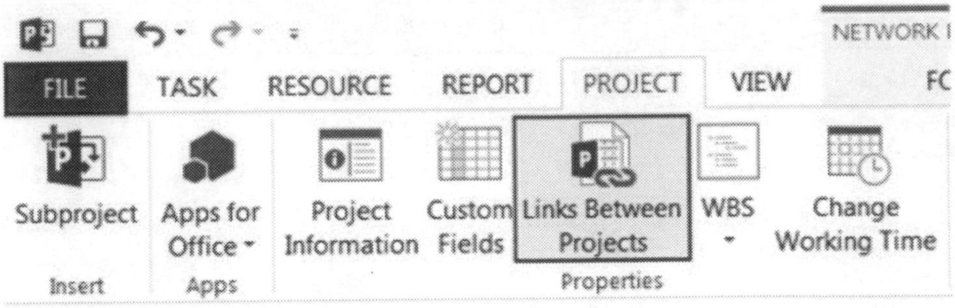

Figure 1-4: Links Between Projects button.

Selecting this button will display the **Links Between Projects** dialog box, which has two tabs. The **External Predecessors** tab shows you which tasks in the project have predecessor tasks in other projects. The **External Successors** tab shows you which tasks in the project have successor tasks in other projects. For example, in the following image, the project has one external predecessor: there is an FS dependency between Subproject Task 2C (which is in another project) and Master Project Task 0A (which is in this project).

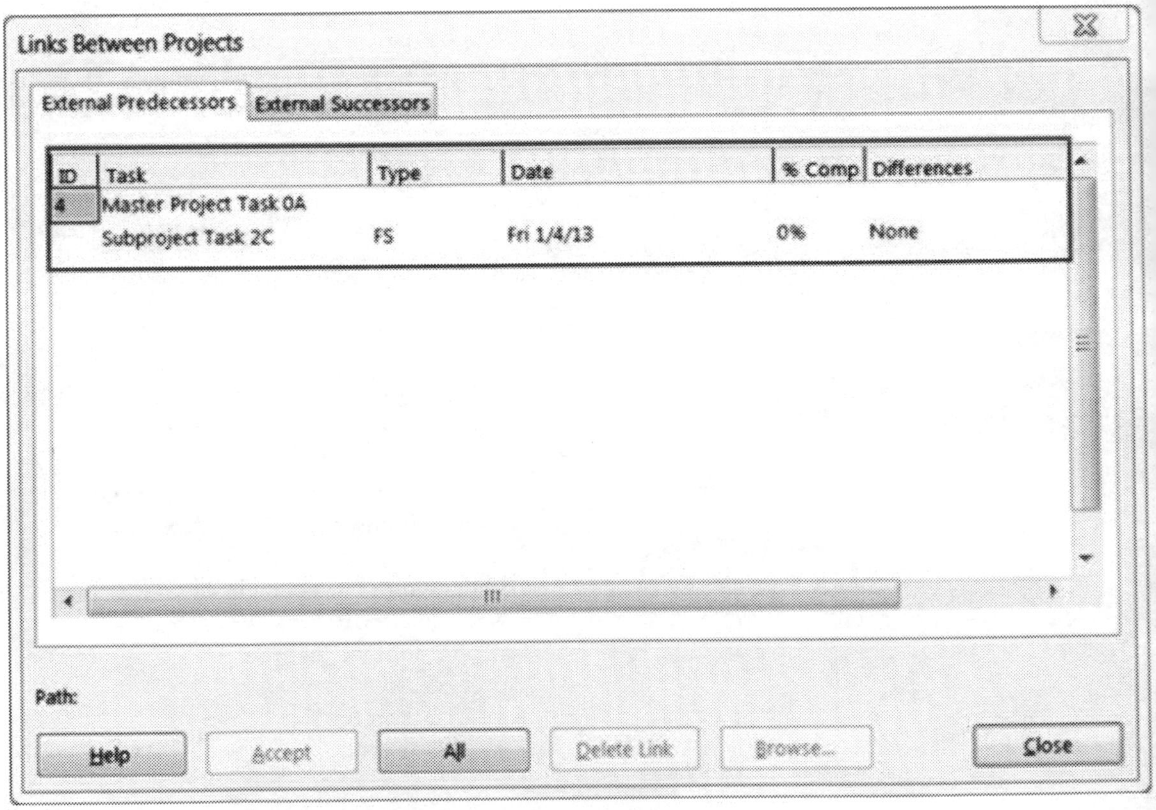

Figure 1-5: Links Between Projects dialog box.

> **Note:** The **Links Between Projects** dialog box will be automatically displayed whenever you open a project file that has tasks with unsynchronized links to tasks in other projects. This gives you the opportunity to review any differences. You can use the buttons at the bottom of the dialog box to accept a single selected difference or accept all differences shown.

Note: The **Links Between Projects** dialog box will show you task links that exist between the open project file and external project files, but it will NOT show you task links that exist between two or more external project files. For example, the dialog box will show you external task links between Master Project.mpp and Subproject 1.mpp and between Master Project.mpp and Subproject 2.mpp, but it will NOT show you external task links between Subproject 1.mpp Subproject 2.mpp.

Access the Checklist tile on your LogicalCHOICE course screen for reference information and job aids on How to Link Projects

ACTIVITY 1–1
Linking Projects

Data Files

C:\091111Data\Managing the Project Environment\Residential Construction 1.mpp

C:\091111Data\Managing the Project Environment\Commercial Construction 1.mpp

Before You Begin

Microsoft Project Professional 2013 is installed on your computer and activated.

Scenario

You work for a public-private partnership that is planning to construct a new planned community called GreeneCentre in the blighted heart of Greene City. The vision for this new neighborhood is to have everything "young urban pioneers" could want within easy walking or biking distance. You are the project manager for both the residential and commercial construction aspects of the initiative. You currently have separate project plans for each aspect. However, you realize that they could be better managed as a single master project.

1. Create a new blank project file to be the master project.
   a) On the Windows 8 **Start** screen, find the **Project 2013** tile.

   b) Select the **Project 2013** tile.
   c) In the Project 2013 **Welcome Center,** select the **Blank Project** option.

Notice that a new, blank project is displayed in the **Gantt Chart** view.

2. Insert **Residential Construction 1.mpp** and **Commercial Construction 1.mpp** into the new master project as subprojects.

   a) In the Gantt Chart of the blank project, select the first empty row.

   b) Select the **PROJECT** tab on the ribbon.

   c) Select the **Insert Subproject** button.

   d) In the **Insert Project** dialog box, navigate to C:\091111Data\Managing the Project Environment and select **Residential Construction 1.mpp**.

   e) Select the second empty row.

   f) Select the **Insert Subproject** button again.

   g) In the **Insert Project** dialog box, navigate to C:\091111Data\Managing the Project Environment and select **Commercial Construction 1.mpp**.
   Notice that both subprojects are visible in the Gantt Chart of the master project and behave much like summary tasks.

3. Create a dependency between tasks in two subprojects.

   a) In the Gantt Chart of the master project, expand the **Residential Construction** subproject by selecting the arrowhead (⏵) next to the subproject name.

   b) Scroll down to the bottom of the Gantt Chart and also expand the **Commercial Construction** subproject.

   c) In the **Residential Construction** subproject, select row 105, **Complete final inspection for certificate of occupancy.**

   d) Scroll down to the **Commercial Construction** subproject, press the **Ctrl** key, and select row 142, **Obtain certificate of occupancy.**

   e) Select the **TASK** tab on the ribbon.

   f) Find the **Schedule** command group.

   g) Select the **Link the Selected Tasks** button. 🔗

   h) In the right pane of the Gantt Chart, notice that there is now an arrow linking the **Complete final inspection for certificate of occupancy** and **Obtain certificate of occupancy** task bars.

   > **Note:** You may need to scroll or change the zoom level to see the task bars in the right pane.

4. Save the master project.

   a) Select the **FILE** tab on the ribbon.

   b) On the **Backstage**, select **Save As.**

   c) In the **Save As** pane, select **Computer.**

   d) In the **Computer** pane, select **Browse.**

   e) In the **Save As** dialog box, navigate to C:\091111Data\Managing the Project Environment.

   f) In the **File name** text box, type *My Master Construction Project.mpp*

   g) Select **Save** to close the dialog box.

   h) When Project 2013 asks you whether you want to save your changes to **Residential Construction 1.mpp** or **Commercial Construction 1.mpp**, select **Yes to All.**

TOPIC B

Baseline a Project

When you are moving from project planning to project execution, it's a good idea to set a baseline so that you can measure how well your project is performing. In this topic, you'll discuss baselines and how to set them.

Baselines

A *baseline* is a measurement, calculation, or location used as a basis for comparison. A *project baseline* is an approved plan for a project. Normally the project plan is approved by the *project sponsor* (the person in an organization who authorizes, supports, and approves a project). The baseline is a snapshot of the planned scope, time, and cost of a project. As the project is executed, you can compare actual scope, time, and cost against the baseline to measure how the project is performing. Here are some of the questions that can be answered.

Project Area	Monitoring Questions
Scope	• Are we doing the tasks we planned to do? • Are we doing more or different tasks than anticipated? • Are we doing fewer tasks than anticipated?
Time	• Are we behind schedule? • Are we on schedule? • Are we ahead of schedule?
Cost	• Are we under budget? • Are we on budget? • Are we over budget?

If your project is not performing as expected, you can take corrective action to finish the project according to scope, on time, and within budget. This is the monitoring and controlling function of project management.

 Note: To further explore baselining in Project 2013, you can access the LearnTO **Baseline a Project** presentation from the **LearnTO** tile on the LogicalCHOICE Course screen.

Set a Baseline

You can easily set a project baseline by selecting the **PROJECT** tab on the ribbon, finding the **Schedule** command group, selecting the **Set Baseline** button, and selecting the **Set Baseline** option.

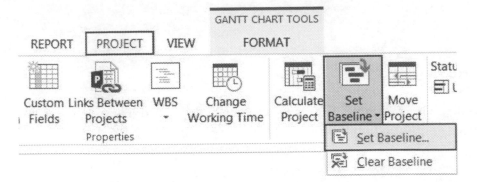

Figure 1-6: Set Baseline button.

Selecting this option will display the **Set Baseline** dialog box. Project 2013 allows you set up to 11 baselines. The best practice is to use Baseline (without a number) for the project plan when it is initially approved, and then to use Baseline 1–10 when the project sponsor approves later changes to the project plan. For example, if the project sponsor approves the addition of several new project tasks a month into project execution, you should capture the change by setting Baseline 1.

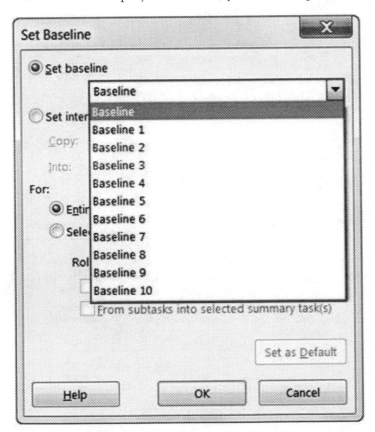

Figure 1-7: Set Baseline dialog box.

> **Note:** You can also use the **Set Baseline** dialog box to take a snapshot of interim plans or baseline selected tasks rather than the entire project. If your project plan has summary tasks and subtasks, you can use the dialog box to specify how you want baselines handled between the summary tasks and subtasks. Finally, you can use **Set as Default** to save your baseline preferences for selected tasks.

> **Note:** As a project manager, you should have a clearly defined process for evaluating and approving changes to the project baseline. The positive and negative effects of potential changes to project scope, time, or cost must be carefully considered before implementing them.

Clear a Baseline

You can also use the **Set Baseline** button to clear a baseline. You may need to clear a baseline if you mistakenly set a baseline or if you have used all 11 baselines and need to reuse some of them.

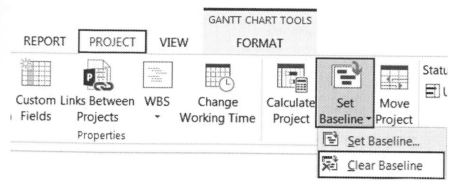

Figure 1–8: Clear Baseline option.

> **Note:** If you find that you are using more than 11 baselines, you may want to take a hard look at your project change-management process. Generally speaking, changes to a project plan should be rare. However, complex or long-term projects often require more changes than projects that are simple or short-term.

Selecting **Clear Baseline** option will display the **Clear Baseline** dialog box.

Clear Baseline

- ⦿ C̲lear baseline plan — Baseline (last saved on Fri 1/4/13) ▾
- ⦾ Clear interim p̲lan — Start1/Finish1 ▾

For ⦿ E̲ntire project ⦾ Selected t̲asks

[OK] [Cancel]

Figure 1–9: Clear Baseline dialog box.

> **Note:** You can also use the **Clear Baseline** dialog box to clear interim plans or clear baselines for selected tasks rather than the entire project.

Variance

In project management, *variance* is the difference between the baseline and actual performance. Variances can occur in scope, time, and cost factors. Small variances at the task level frequently result in large variances at the project level.

Project 2013 includes a number of built-in tables that show you variance. You can access these tables on the **VIEW** tab of the ribbon, in the **Data** command group, in the **Tables** button drop-down menu. The **Cost** table shows variances between planned and actual costs. The **Variance** table shows variances in planned and actual dates and duration. The **Work** table shows variances in planned and actual work.

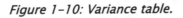

	Task Mode	Task Name	Start	Finish	Baseline Start	Baseline Finish	Start Var.	Finish Var.	Feb 3, '13 S M T W T
0		◢ Commercial Con	Thu 1/1/15	Fri 5/13/16	Thu 1/1/15	Tue 4/26/16	0 days	13 days	
1		◢ General Condi	Thu 1/1/15	Mon 2/2/15	Thu 1/1/15	Fri 1/23/15	0 days	6 days	
2		Receive not	Thu 1/1/15	Mon 1/5/15	Thu 1/1/15	Mon 1/5/15	0 days	0 days	
3		Submit bon	Tue 1/6/15	Tue 1/27/15	Tue 1/6/15	Wed 1/7/15	0 days	14 days	
4		Prepare anc	Wed 1/28/15	Thu 1/29/15	Thu 1/8/15	Fri 1/9/15	14 days	14 days	
5		Prepare anc	Fri 1/30/15	Mon 2/2/15	Mon 1/12/15	Tue 1/13/15	14 days	14 days	
6		Obtain buil	Tue 1/6/15	Fri 1/9/15	Tue 1/6/15	Fri 1/9/15	0 days	0 days	
7		Submit prel	Mon 1/12/15	Fri 1/23/15	Mon 1/12/15	Fri 1/23/15	0 days	0 days	
8		Submit mor	Tue 1/6/15	Tue 1/6/15	Tue 1/6/15	Tue 1/6/15	0 days	0 days	
9		◢ Long Lead Proc	Wed 1/7/15	Tue 4/14/15	Wed 1/7/15	Tue 4/14/15	0 days	0 days	
10		Submit shop	Wed 1/7/15	Tue 1/20/15	Wed 1/7/15	Tue 1/20/15	0 days	0 days	
11		Submit shop	Mon 1/26/15	Fri 2/6/15	Mon 1/26/15	Fri 2/6/15	0 days	0 days	
12		Submit shop	Mon 1/26/15	Fri 2/6/15	Mon 1/26/15	Fri 2/6/15	0 days	0 days	
13		Submit shop	Mon 1/26/15	Fri 2/6/15	Mon 1/26/15	Fri 2/6/15	0 days	0 days	
14		Submit shop	Mon 1/26/15	Fri 2/6/15	Mon 1/26/15	Fri 2/6/15	0 days	0 days	

Figure 1-10: Variance table.

Access the Checklist tile on your LogicalCHOICE course screen for reference information and job aids on How to Baseline a Project

ACTIVITY 1-2
Baselining a Project

Before You Begin
My Master Construction Project.mpp is open.

Scenario
The planning phase of the GreeneCentre initiative is drawing to a close and implementation will soon begin. Your project sponsor has approved your master construction project plan. You know that you need to set a baseline for the project.

1. Using the master project file you created previously, set a baseline for the project.
   a) Select the **PROJECT** tab on the ribbon.
   b) Find the **Schedule** command group.
   c) Select the **Set Baseline** button.

   d) From the drop-down list, select the **Set Baseline** option. Set Baseline...
   e) In the **Set Baseline** dialog box, verify that the **Set baseline** option is selected and that **Baseline** appears in the drop-down field.
   f) Select **OK** to close the dialog box.

2. Verify that the baseline is set.
   a) Select the **Set Baseline** button again.

   b) From the drop-down list, select the **Set Baseline** option again.
   c) In the **Set Baseline** dialog box, verify that a save day and date appear next to **Baseline** in the drop-down field.

   > Baseline (last saved on Thu 1/24/13)   ▼

   d) Select **Cancel** to close the dialog box without making any changes.

3. Save and close the project file.

TOPIC C

Work with Custom Fields

Microsoft Project Professional 2013 comes packed with hundreds of fields for capturing information about project tasks and resources. However, there may be situations in which you need additional or different data fields than those provided. In this topic, you'll see how to add custom fields to a project.

Custom Fields

Custom fields are data fields that you can configure for your unique project or organizational needs. Dozens of these custom fields already exist as placeholders in Project 2013, just waiting for you to make them your own.

There are several ways to use custom fields:

- You can insert data that is important to your organization.
- You can write formulas that will perform calculations.
- You can add lookup tables to make data entry more accurate.
- You can build graphical indicators to call attention to important items.
- You can create hierarchical coding structures.

Add Custom Fields

You can create a custom field by selecting the **PROJECT** tab on the ribbon, finding the **Properties** command group, and selecting the **Custom Fields** button.

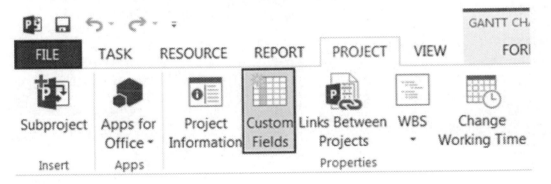

Figure 1-11: Custom Fields button.

The **Custom Fields** dialog box will display.

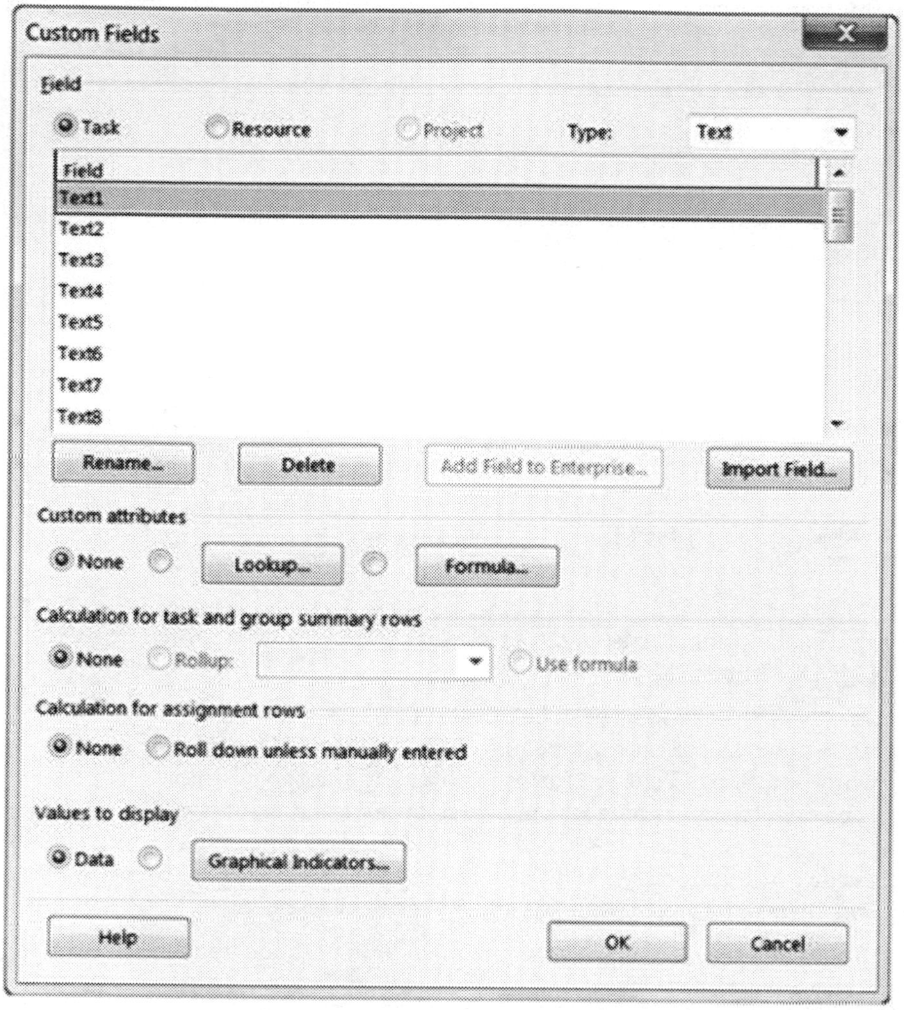

Figure 1-12: Custom Fields dialog box.

Custom Field Options

The **Custom Fields** dialog box gives you many options for configuring custom fields.

Section of Dialog Box	Options and Functions
Field	

Section of Dialog Box	Options and Functions
	  Select the **Task** option to customize a task field. Select the **Resource** option to customize a resource field. Regardless of whether you want to customize a task or resource field, from the **Type** drop-down list, select the type of field (**Cost, Date, Duration, Finish, Flag, Number, Start, Text** or **Outline Code**) you want to customize. A fixed number of each type of field is assigned to both tasks and resources. For example, 30 customizable text fields are set aside for tasks, and 30 customizable text fields are set aside for resources. Similarly, 10 customizable cost fields are set aside for tasks, and 10 customizable cost fields are set aside for resources. Select **Rename** to rename fields from their default names to something more descriptive of their functions. Select **Delete** to remove a customized field. When you do this, you are actually returning the field to its pre-customized state.
Custom attributes	 Select the **Lookup** option to create a lookup table. A lookup table is useful when you want to be able to populate a field by selecting a value from a drop-down list. For example, you might create a lookup table called *Priority Code* with the values *High, Medium,* and *Low.* When you select the **Lookup** button, an **Edit Lookup Table** dialog box will be displayed where you can enter the data for your lookup table and set parameters for the table. Select the **Formula** option to create a formula field. A formula is useful when you want Project 2013 to perform a calculation for you. When you select the **Formula** button, the **Formula** dialog box will be displayed for you to compile your formula.
Calculation for task and group summary rows	

Section of Dialog Box	Options and Functions
	Select the **Rollup** option and select a rollup option from the drop-down list to customize how Project 2013 calculates task and group summary rows. In project management, to *rollup* means to include lower-level project information at higher levels of the project.
	Select the **Use formula** option if you want to use the formula field you created for the rollup calculation.
Calculation for assignment rows	Calculation for assignment rows ◉ None ○ Roll down unless manually entered
	Select the **Roll down unless manually entered** option if you want the values of the customized field to be spread evenly across each assignment.
Values to display	Values to display ◉ Data ○ [Graphical Indicators...]
	Select the **Data** option to see the actual information entered into a field.
	Select the **Graphical Indicators** option and then select the **Graphical Indicators** button to apply graphical indicators to your custom field. When you select the **Graphical Indicators** button, the **Graphical Indicators** dialog box will be displayed, where you can select criteria for what to display and when.

> **Caution:** Be careful with the **Delete** option because deleting a customized field will also delete any project data entered into the custom field.

View Custom Fields

You can view your customized fields, and enter data into them, by selecting the **Custom Fields** tab of the **Task Information** or **Resource Information** dialog box.

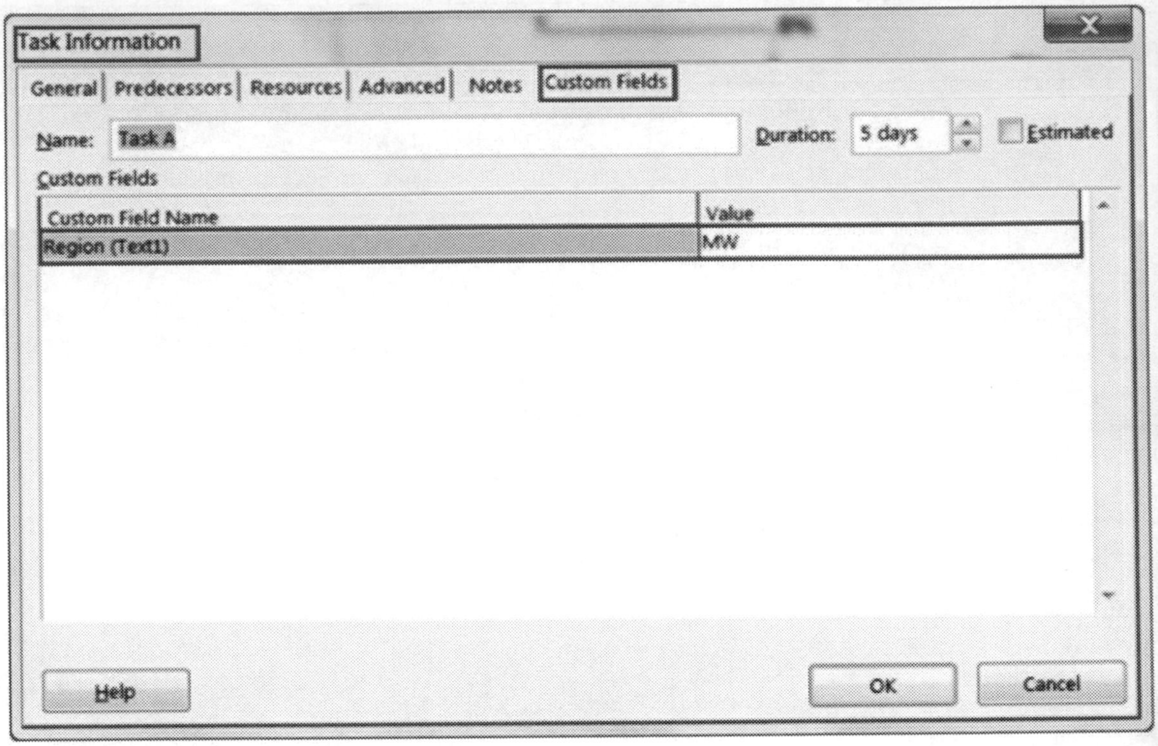

Figure 1-13: Custom field with lookup table in the Task Information dialog box.

You can add customized fields as columns in views such as **Gantt Chart** and **Resource Sheet.** If your custom field includes a graphical indicator, it will be displayed in the column.

Figure 1-14: Custom field with graphical indicator in Gantt Chart view.

Lookup Tables

As stated previously, when you select the **Lookup** button in the **Custom Fields** dialog box, the **Edit Lookup Table** dialog box will open. Use this dialog box to enter the data for your lookup table and set parameters for it.

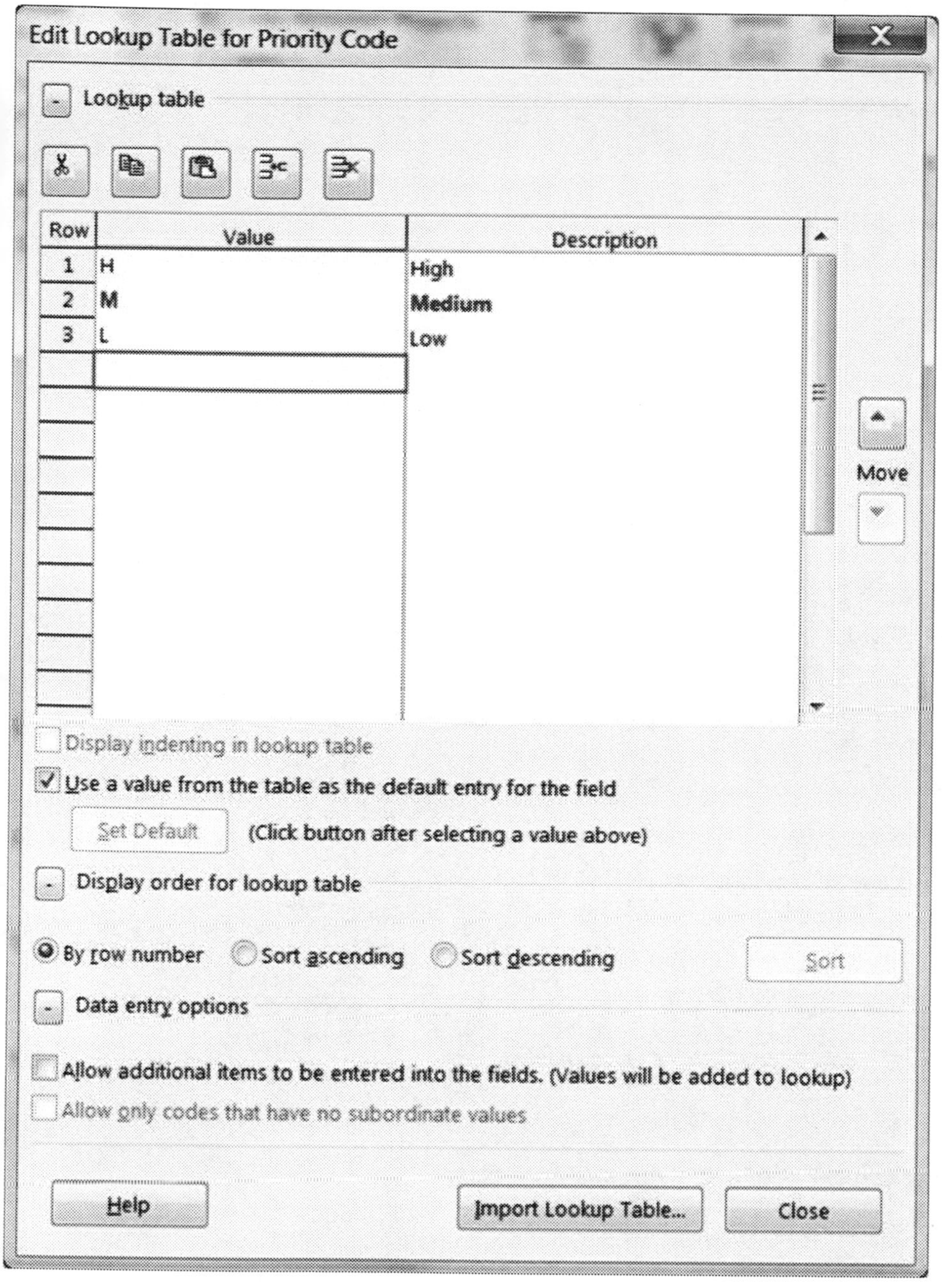

Figure 1–15: Lookup Table dialog box.

For example, in the figure shown, a project manager is creating a lookup table for the custom task text field named **Priority Code.** She entered short codes in the **Value** column and an explanation of those codes in the **Description** column. She also chose **M** as the default entry for the field.

> **Note:** There are several options you can specify for a lookup table in the **Edit Lookup Table** dialog box. These include selecting a value from the table as the default entry value, sorting the values in different ways, and allowing values not listed in the table to be entered.

Formulas

As mentioned earlier, you can create custom fields that contain formulas. Formulas allow you to generate new values from project data that are not readily visible in pre-existing fields. For example, perhaps you would like to know the number of days between the current date and the finish date of the tasks in your schedule. Project 2013 does not have a built-in field containing this information. So, you could create a custom number field with a formula that provides it.

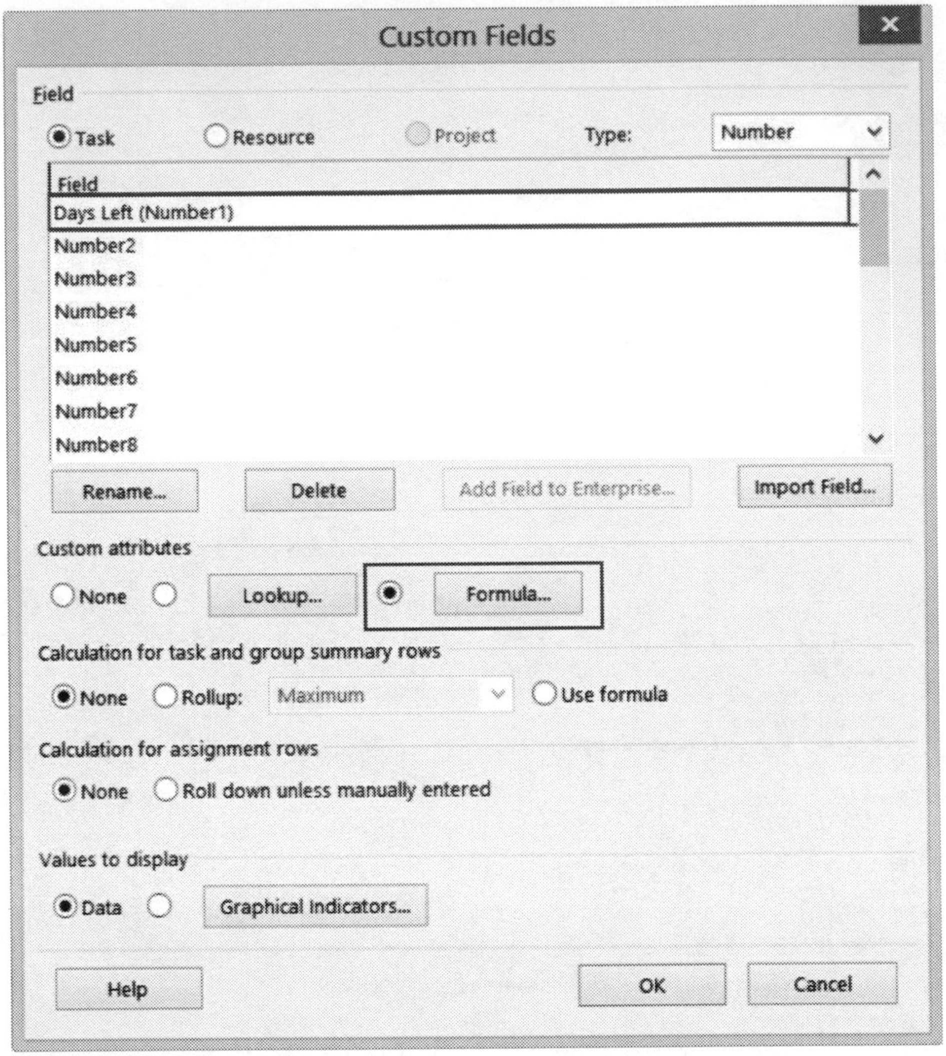

Figure 1-16: Custom number field with a formula for a task.

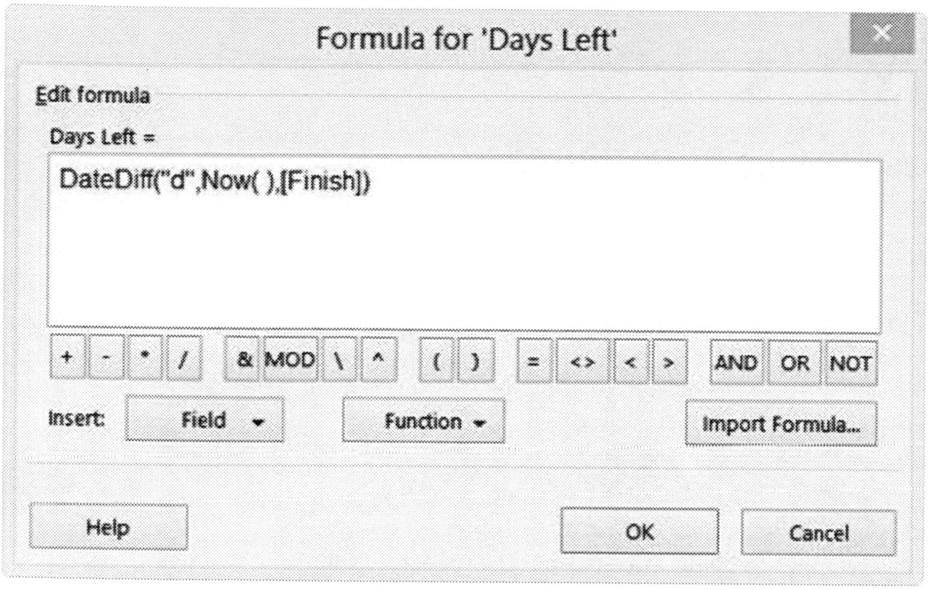

Formula for 'Days Left'   ✕

Edit formula

Days Left =

> DateDiff("d",Now( ),[Finish])

| + | − | * | / | | & | MOD | \ | ^ | | (|) | | = | <> | < | > | | AND | OR | NOT |

Insert: [Field ▾]   [Function ▾]   [Import Formula...]

[Help]   [OK]   [Cancel]

Figure 1–17: Formula dialog box.

There are three methods for entering a formula in the **Formula** dialog box. You can:

- Type the formula.
- Construct the formula using the field, function, and operator controls provided.
- Import the formula from another Project file.

> Access the Checklist tile on your LogicalCHOICE course screen for reference information and job aids on **How to Add Custom Fields**

ACTIVITY 1–3
Working with Custom Fields

Data Files

C:\091111Data\Managing the Project Environment\Commercial Construction 1.mpp

Before You Begin

Microsoft Project Professional 2013 is open.

Scenario

You will soon be choosing contract resources for the commercial construction project of the GreeneCentre initiative. One of the grants your public-private partnership was awarded for this part of the GreeneCentre initiative requires that a certain percentage of contractors meet one or more specific criteria. You want to add a custom lookup table to your commercial construction plan so that you can easily capture this information about each contractor. Since you are creating a custom field, you also decide to add a formula field so that you can determine the number of days between the current date and the finish date for each task in your schedule.

1. Open C:\091111Data\Managing the Project Environment\Commercial Construction 1.mpp.

2. Rename the **Resources Text1** field to *Grant Criteria*
   a) Select the **PROJECT** tab on the ribbon.
   b) Find the **Properties** command group.
   c) Select the **Custom Fields** button.

   d) In the **Custom Fields** dialog box, select the **Resource** option.
   e) In the **Type** drop-down list, make sure **Text** is selected.

   f) In the **Field** section, make sure **Text1** is selected.
   g) Select **Rename.**
   h) In the **Rename Field** dialog box, type *Grant Criteria* as the new name for the field.
   i) Select **OK** to close the **Rename Field** dialog box.
   j) Select **OK** to close the **Custom Fields** dialog box.

3. Make the **Grant Criteria** custom field into a lookup table.
   a) Select the **Custom Fields** button again.
   b) In the **Custom Fields** dialog box, select the **Resource** option and make sure the **Grant Criteria (Text1)** custom field is selected.

c) In the **Custom attributes** section, select the **Lookup** button. [Lookup...]
d) In the **Edit Lookup Table for Grant Criteria** dialog box, select the first cell of the **Value** column and type *W*
e) Select the first cell of the **Description** column and type *Women Owned*
f) Select the second cell of the **Value** column and type *M*
g) Select the second cell of the **Description** column and type *Minority Owned*
h) Select the third cell of the **Value** column and type *V*
i) Select the third cell of the **Description** column and type *Veteran Owned*
j) Select the fourth cell of the **Value** column and type *>1*
k) Select the fourth cell of the **Description** column and type *More Than One*

Edit Lookup Table for Grant Criteria

Lookup table

Row	Value	Description
1	W	Women Owned
2	M	Minority Owned
3	V	Veteran Owned
4	>1	More Than One

Move

☐ Display indenting in lookup table
☐ Use a value from the table as the default entry for the field
   [Set Default]   (Click button after selecting a value above)

Display order for lookup table

◉ By row number   ○ Sort ascending   ○ Sort descending   [Sort]

Data entry options

☐ Allow additional items to be entered into the fields. (Values will be added to lookup)
☐ Allow only codes that have no subordinate values

[Help]   [Import Lookup Table...]   [Close]

l) Select **Close** to close the **Edit Lookup Table for Grant Criteria** dialog box.
m) Select **OK** to close the **Custom Fields** dialog box.

4. Add a graphical indicator to the **Grant Criteria** custom field.

a) Select the **Custom Fields** button again.

b) In the **Custom Fields** dialog box, select the **Resource** option and make sure the **Grant Criteria (Text1)** custom field is selected.

c) In the **Values to display** section, select the **Graphical Indicators** button.

d) In the **Graphical Indicators** dialog box, select the first cell of the **Test for 'Grant Criteria'** column and select **equals** from the drop-down list.

e) Select the first cell of the **Value(s)** column and type *W*

f) Select the first cell of the **Image** column and select a half-filled circle ◓ from the drop-down list.

g) Select the second cell of the **Test for 'Grant Criteria'** column and select **equals** from the drop-down list.

h) Select the second cell of the **Value(s)** column and type *M*

i) Select the second cell of the **Image** column and select a half-filled circle from the drop-down list.

j) Select the third cell of the **Test for 'Grant Criteria'** column and select **equals** from the drop-down list.

k) Select the third cell of the **Value(s)** column and type *V*

l) Select the third cell of the **Image** column and select a half-filled circle from the drop-down list.

m) Select the fourth cell of the **Test for 'Grant Criteria'** column and select **equals** from the drop-down list.

n) Select the fourth cell of the **Value(s)** column and type *>1*

o) Select the fourth cell of the **Image** column and select a solid circle ● from the drop-down list.

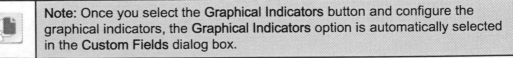

p) Select **OK** to close the **Graphical Indicators** dialog box.

q) Verify that, in the **Values to display** section, the **Graphical Indicators** option is now selected.

> **Note:** Once you select the **Graphical Indicators** button and configure the graphical indicators, the **Graphical Indicators** option is automatically selected in the **Custom Fields** dialog box.

r) Select **OK** to close the **Custom Fields** dialog box.

5. Create a custom formula field.

a) Reopen the **Custom Fields** dialog box.

b) If necessary, select the **Task** option. In the **Type** field, select **Number**.

c) Rename the **Task Number1** field to *Days Left*

Custom Fields

Field

○ Task ○ Resource ○ Project Type: Number

Field
Days Left (Number1)
Number2
Number3
Number4
Number5
Number6
Number7
Number8

Rename...   Delete   Add Field to Enterprise...   Import Field...

Custom attributes

○ None   ○ Lookup...   ○ Formula...

Calculation for task and group summary rows

○ None   ○ Rollup: Maximum   ○ Use formula

Calculation for assignment rows

○ None   ○ Roll down unless manually entered

Values to display

○ Data   ○ Graphical Indicators...

Help   OK   Cancel

d) Select the **Formula** button.

e) In the **Formula** dialog box, select the **Function** button, choose **Date / Time** from the drop-down, and select the **DateDiff** option.

Formula for 'Days Left'

Edit formula

Days Left =

DateDiff(interval, date1, date2, firstdayofweek, firstweekofyear)

+ - * / & MOD \ ^ ( ) = <> < > AND OR NOT

Insert: Field ▾   Function ▾   Import Formula...

Help   OK   Cancel

f)   In the formula, select **interval** with the mouse pointer. Replace it by typing *"d"* for day.

g)   In the formula, select **date1** with the mouse pointer. Replace it by selecting the **Function** button, choosing **Date / Time** from the drop-down, and selecting the **Now()** option.

h)   In the formula, select **date2** with the mouse pointer. Replace it by selecting the **Field** button, choosing **Date** from the drop-down, and selecting the **Finish** option.

i)   In the formula, highlight **, firstdayofweek, firstweekofyear** and delete the text by clicking the **Delete** button. If necessary, delete all extraneous spaces in the formula.

Formula for 'Days Left'

Edit formula

Days Left =

DateDiff("d",Now( ),[Finish])

| + | - | * | / | | & | MOD | \ | ^ | | (|) | | = | <> | < | > | | AND | OR | NOT |

Insert: Field ▼   Function ▼   Import Formula...

Help   OK   Cancel

j)   Select **OK** to close the **Formula** dialog box.

k)   If necessary, in the **Microsoft Project** dialog box about replacing all the data in the **Days Left** field, select **OK**.

l)   Select **OK** to close the **Custom Fields** dialog box.

6. Verify that the **View Bar** is visible on the left side of the Project 2013 interface. If it isn't, make it visible. (You learned how to do this in *Microsoft® Project 2013: Part 1.*)

7. Add a **Grant Criteria** column to the **Resource Sheet**.

a)   Find and select the **Resource Sheet** button on the **View Bar**.

 Note: You may need to select the down arrow at the bottom of the **View Bar** to find the **Resource Sheet** button.

b)   In the **Resource Sheet** view, select the **Material** column.

c)   Right-click and select **Insert Column**.

d)   In the **Type Column Name** field, type *Grant Criteria* and press **Enter**. Verify that the view contains a new column titled **Grant Criteria**.

	ⓘ	Resource Name	Type ▼	Grant Criteria ▼	Material ▼	Initials ▼	Group ▼	Max. ▼
1		G.C. General Management	Work	▼		G		100%
2		G.C. Project Management	Work			G		100%
3		G.C. Procurement	Work			G		100%
4		G.C. Scheduler	Work			G		100%
5		G.C. Accounting	Work			G		100%
6		G.C. Superintendent	Work			G		100%
7		G.C. Survey Crew	Work			G		100%
8		G.C. Rough Carpenter Crew	Work			G		100%
9		G.C. Labor Crew	Work			G		100%
10		G.C. Concrete Crew	Work			G		100%
11		G.C. Finish Carpenter Crew	Work			G		100%

Note: If you select a cell in the **Grant Criteria** column, select the down arrow, and select an option, Project 2013 will convert your choice into the corresponding graphical indicator.

8. Add a **Days Left** column to the **Gantt Chart**.
   a) Select the **Gantt Chart** button on the **View Bar**.
   b) In the **Gantt Chart** view, select the **Predecessors** column.
   c) Right-click and select **Insert Column**.
   d) In the **Type Column Name** field, type *Days Left* and press **Enter**. Verify that the view contains a new column titled **Days Left**.

	ⓘ	Task Mode ▾	Task Name ▾	Duration ▾	Start ▾	Finish ▾	Days Left ▾	Predecessors
3		⬚	Submit bond and insurance documents	4 days	Tue 1/6/15	Tue 1/27/15	588	2
4		⬚	Prepare and submit project schedule	2 days	Wed 1/28/15	Thu 1/29/15	590	3
5		⬚	Prepare and submit schedule of	2 days	Fri 1/30/15	Mon 2/2/15	594	4
6		⬚	Obtain building permits	4 days	Tue 1/6/15	Fri 1/9/15	570	2

 Note: To see values in this column, you may need to expand subtasks and scroll vertically. The values may be rather large because the formula uses your computer's current date as the **Now** value for the calculation.

9. Save the file in C:\091111Data\Managing the Project Environment as *My Commercial Construction 1.mpp* and then close the file.

TOPIC D

Change Project Options

There is a difference between managing the environment of a specific project file and managing the environment of the Microsoft Project Professional 2013 application. You can use the commands on the **PROJECT** tab to change the settings for a specific project, but you must go to the **Backstage** to change the settings for Project 2013 as a whole.

Backstage

As its name implies, the **Backstage** is a behind-the-scenes section of Project 2013 (and other applications in the Office 2013 suite). You can access the **Backstage** by selecting the **FILE** tab on the ribbon. In *Microsoft® Project 2013: Part 1,* you used several tabs on the **Backstage**—including **Save As**, **Print**, **Share**, and **Export**. If you select the **Options** tab on the **Backstage**, the **Project Options** dialog box will open.

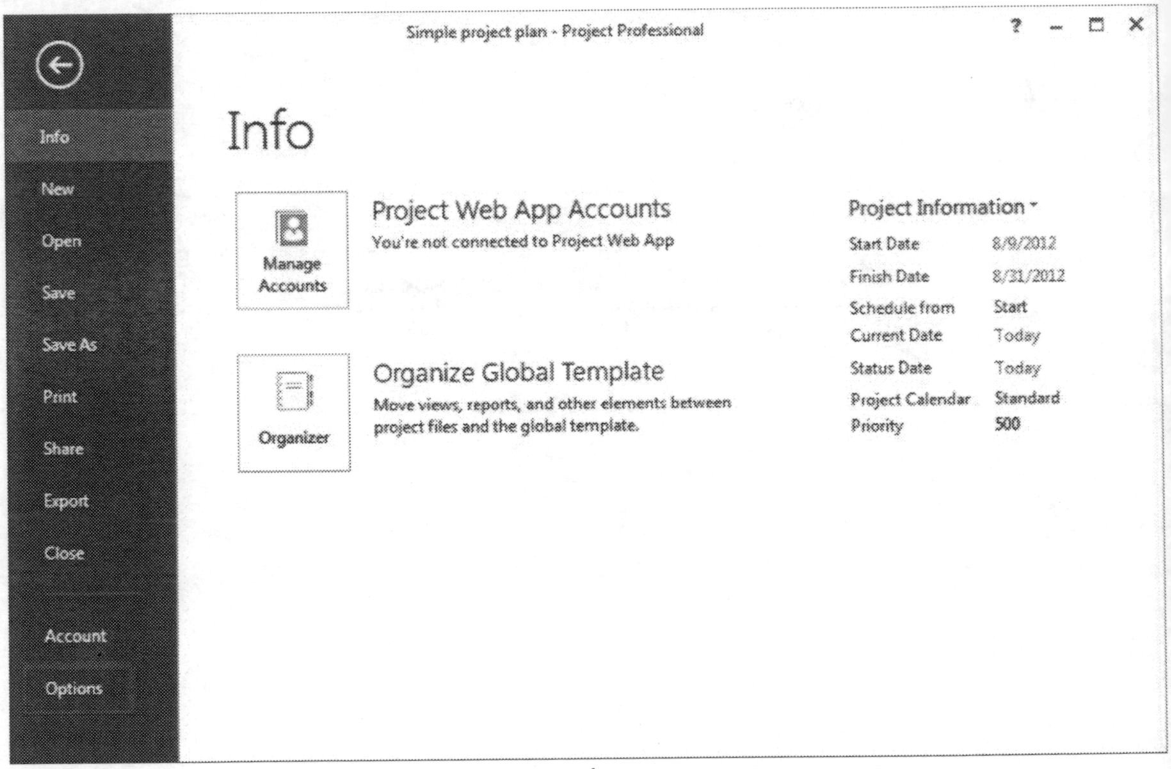

Figure 1-18: The Backstage.

General Project Options

The **Project Options** dialog box is packed with a multitude of options grouped into eleven screens. On the **General** screen you can change:

- How **ScreenTips** are displayed
- The default view
- The date format
- Your user name
- Your initials
- The Office background

- The Office theme
- Whether the **Start** screen displays when the application opens

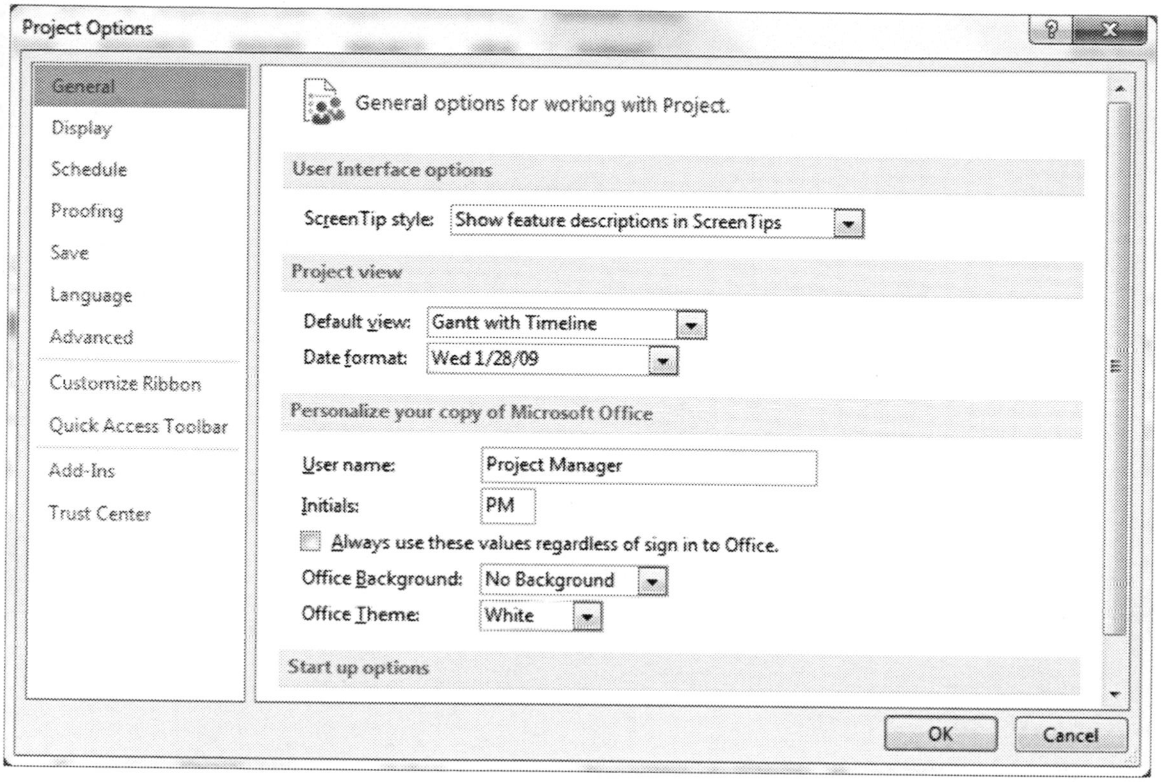

Figure 1-19: General options.

Display Project Options

On the **Display** screen you can change:

- The calendar type (Gregorian, Hijri, Thai Buddhist)
- Currency settings
- Whether or not to show several types of indicators and option buttons

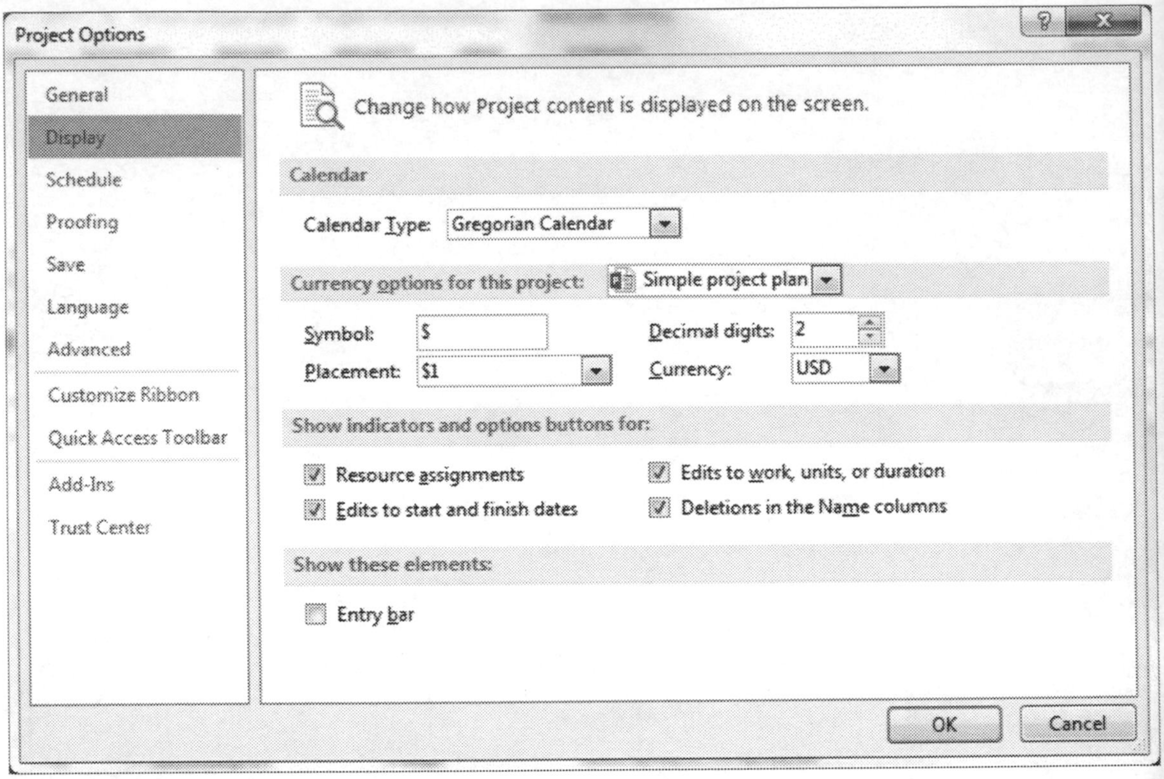

Figure 1-20: Display options.

Schedule Project Options

On the **Schedule** screen you can change:

- The first day of the week
- The fiscal year
- Daily start and end times
- Hours per day and week
- Days per month
- How assignment units are displayed
- Whether new tasks are automatically or manually scheduled
- Whether auto scheduled tasks begin on the project start date or calendar date
- Which time units are used for task duration and work
- The default task type (Fixed Units, Fixed Duration, or Fixed Work)
- Whether alerts and suggestions are displayed
- Calculation options

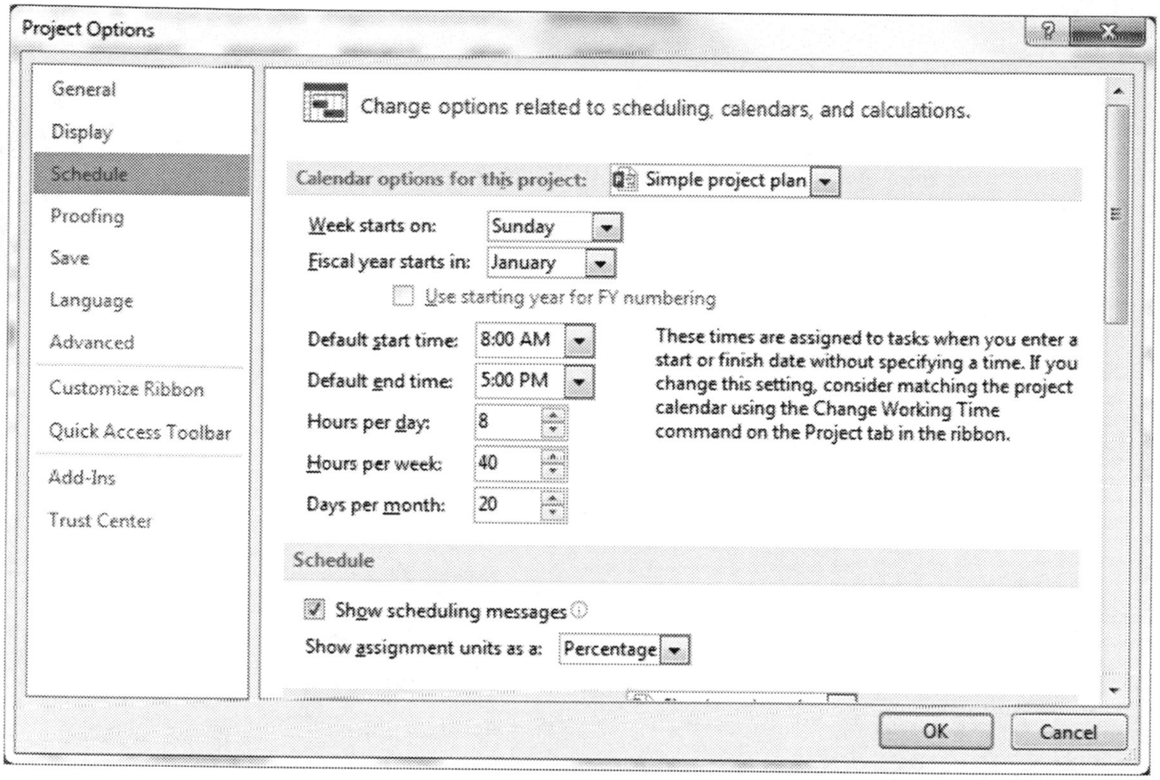

Figure 1-21: Schedule options.

Proofing Project Options

On the **Proofing** screen you can change:

- AutoCorrect options
- Spelling settings
- Which fields are spell checked

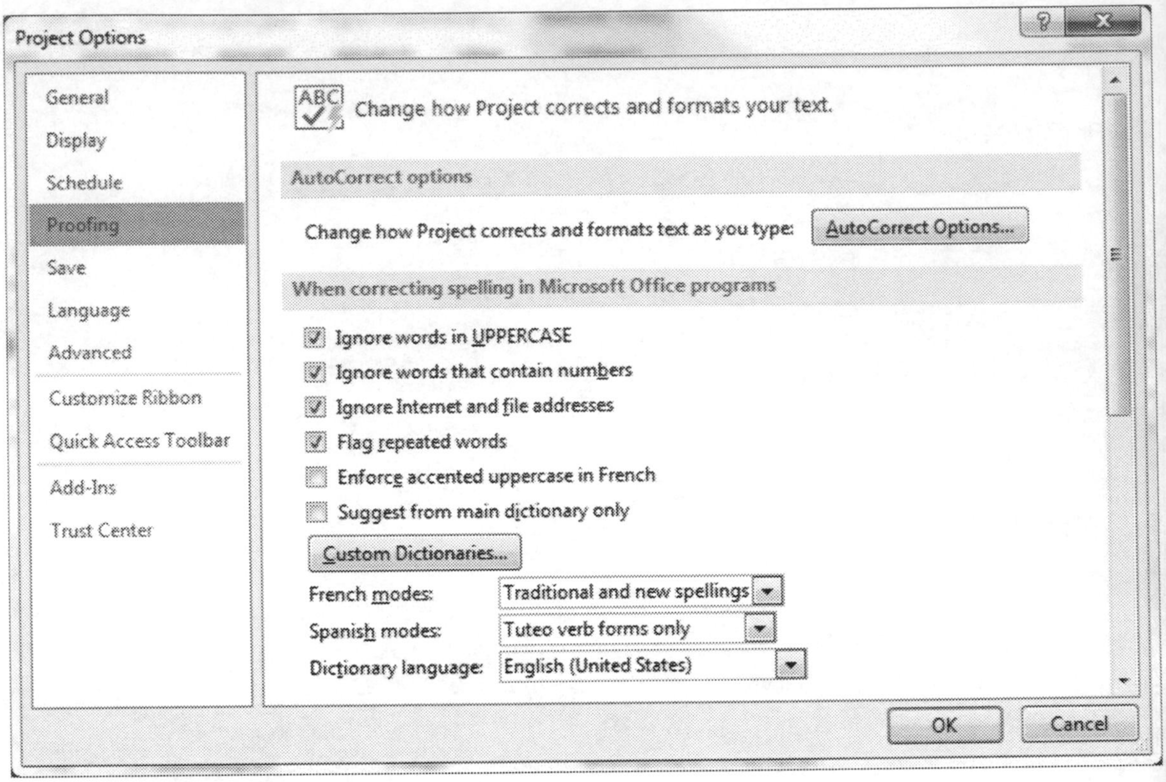

Figure 1-22: Proofing options.

Save Project Options

On the **Save** screen you can change:

- The default file type
- Where files are saved
- Auto save options

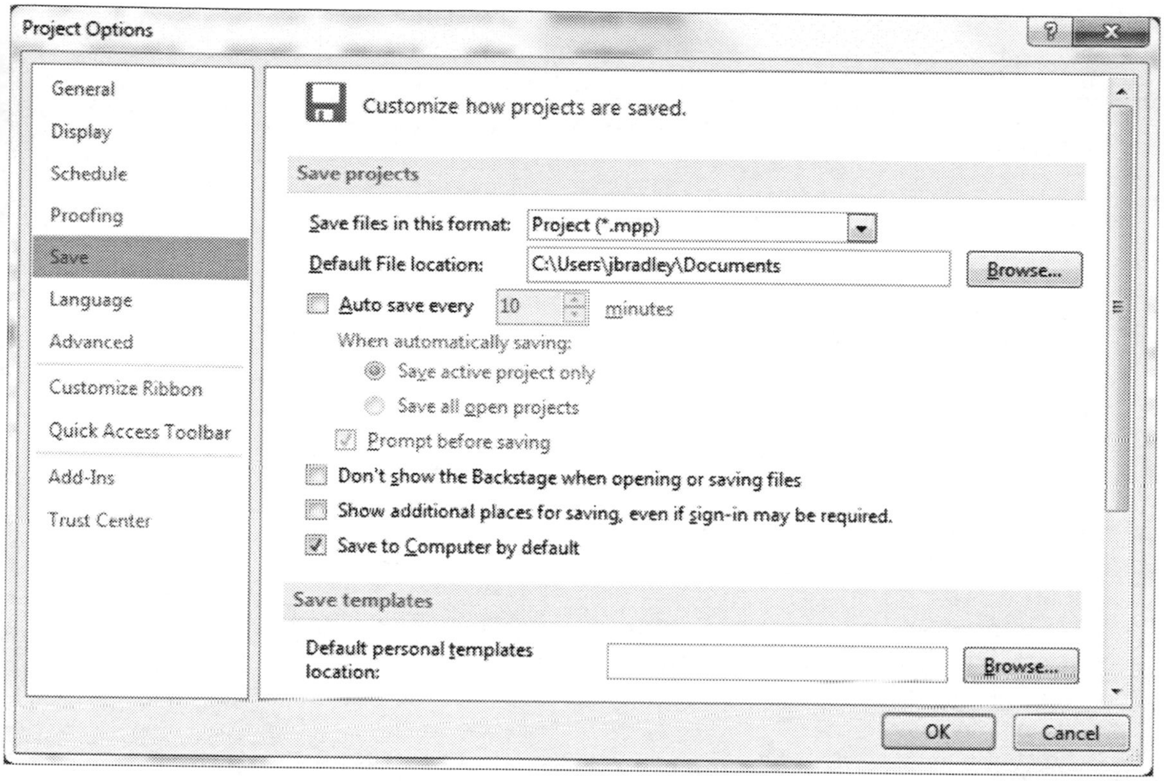

Figure 1-23: Save options.

Language Project Options

On the **Language** screen you can change which language(s) are used for spell check, the program interface, and **Help**.

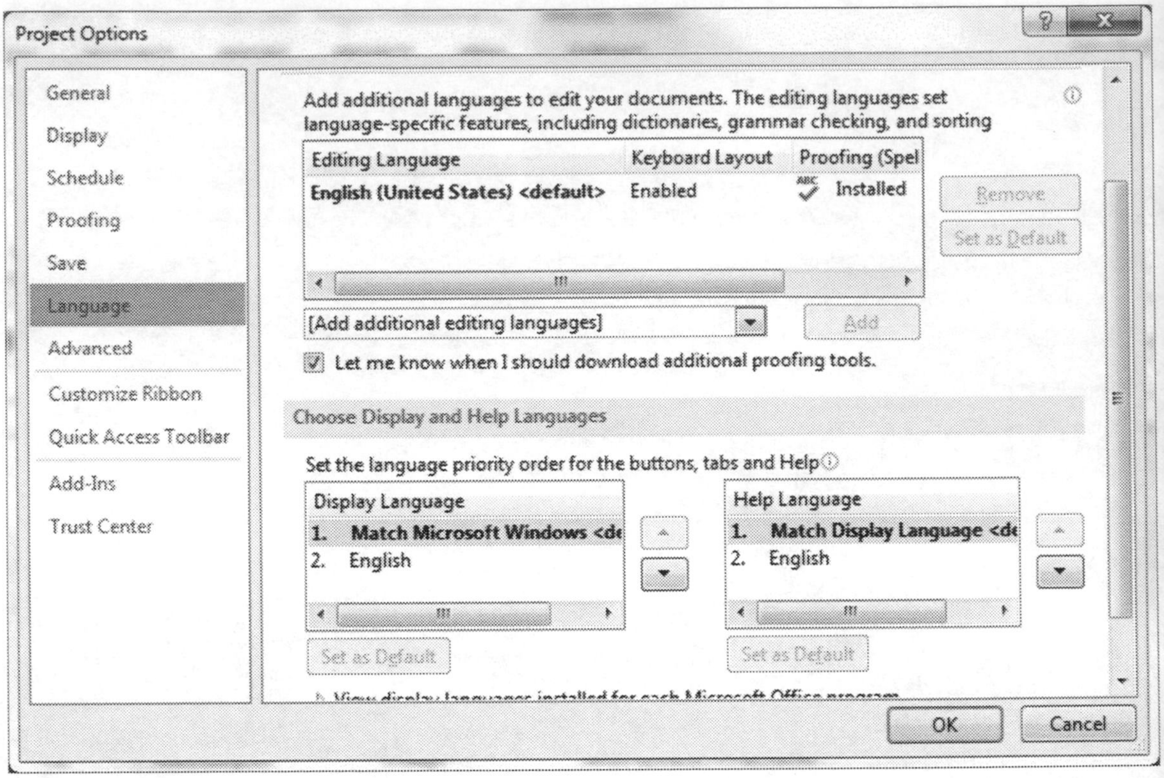

Figure 1-24: Language options.

Advanced Project Options

On the **Advanced** screen you can change:

- What happens when you open Project 2013 or start a new project
- Planning Wizard options
- Standard and overtime rates for new resources and tasks
- Editing options
- Abbreviations for time units
- Options for linking projects
- Earned value settings
- Advanced calculation options

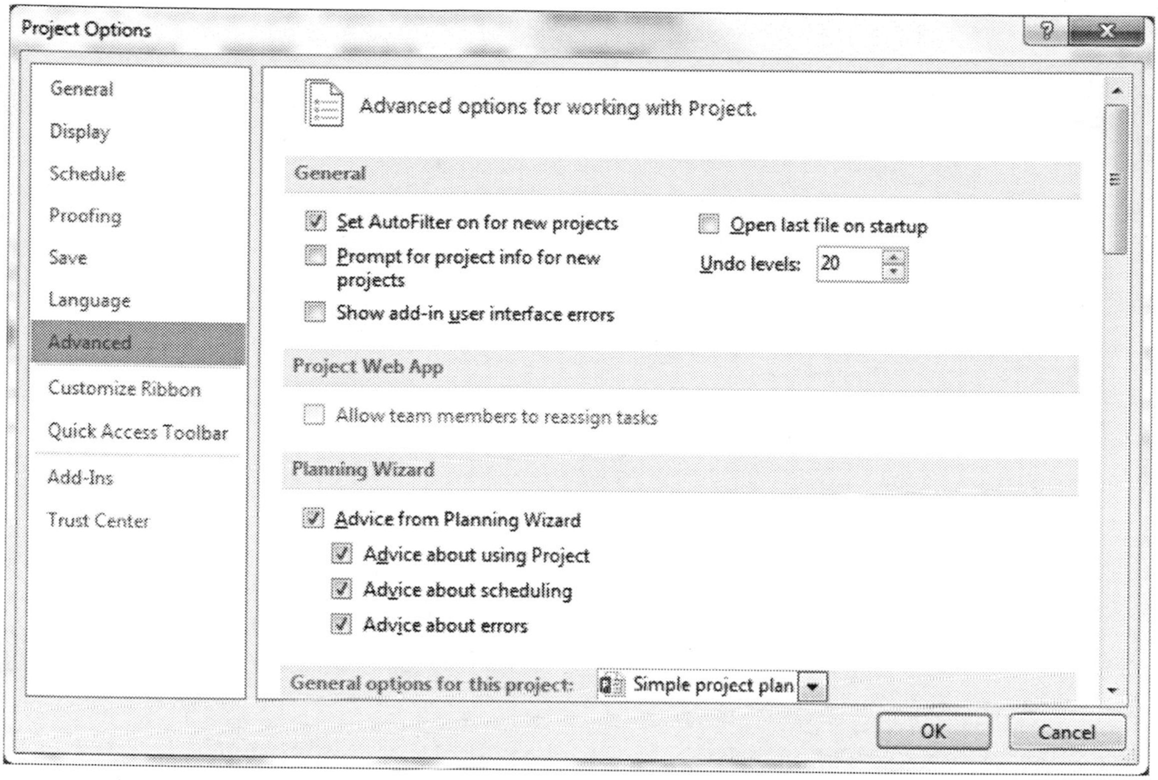

Figure 1-25: Advanced options.

Customize Ribbon

On the **Customize Ribbon** screen you can change the configuration of the ribbon. The left column lists the available tabs, groups, and commands. The right column lists the current configuration of the ribbon. Using the buttons on this page, you can:

* Add new tabs and groups
* Add items from the left column to the right column
* Remove items from the right column to the left column
* Move items up or down in the right column
* Reset customizations

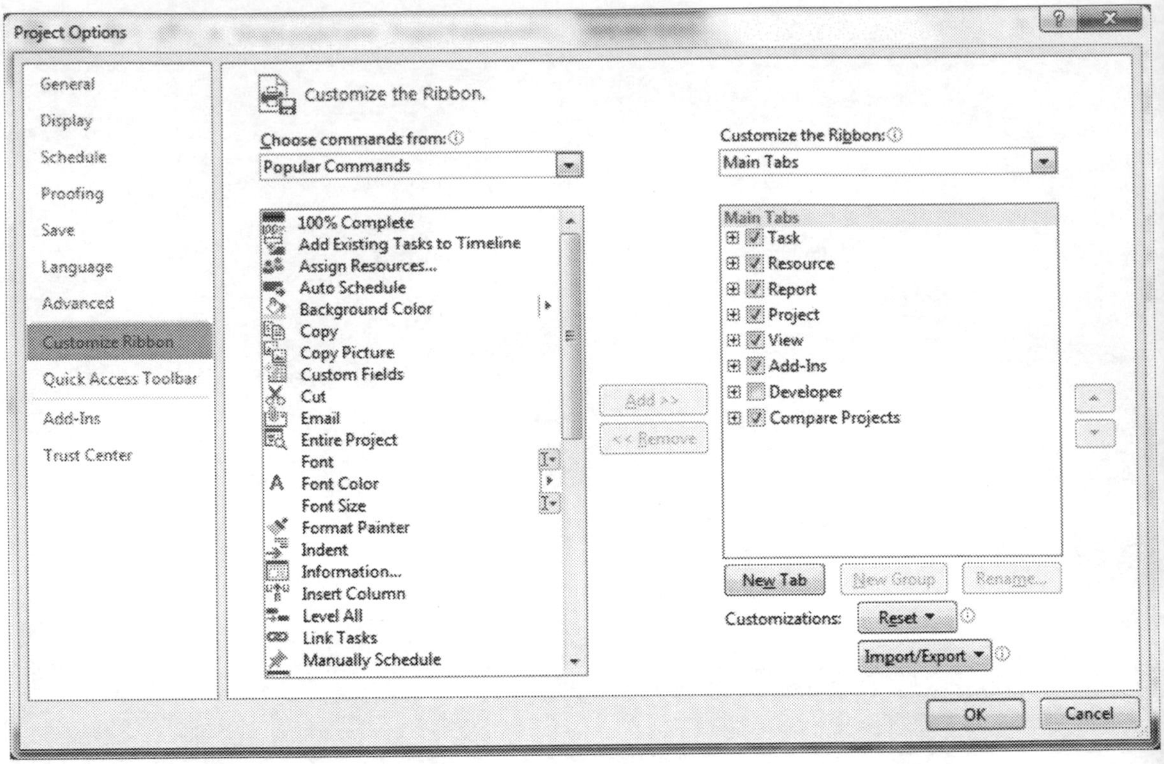

Figure 1-26: Customize ribbon.

If you create a new tab, Project 2013 will also automatically create a new group under the new tab. Before you can add a command from the left column to the right column, you must create a new group in a new or existing tab. If you reset the ribbon, the **Quick Access Toolbar** will reset as well.

Quick Access Toolbar

On the **Customize Ribbon** screen you can change the configuration of the **Quick Access Toolbar**. This page works much like the **Customize Ribbon** page.

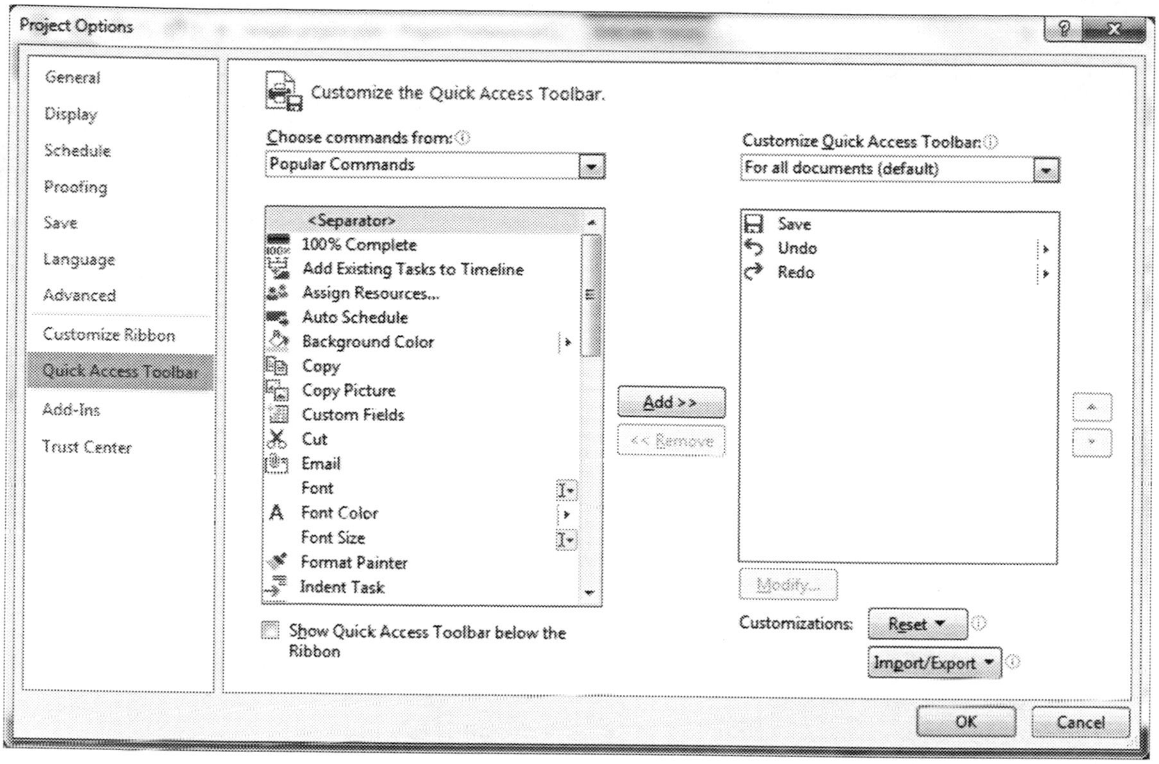

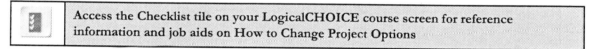

Figure 1-27: Quick access toolbar.

Access the Checklist tile on your LogicalCHOICE course screen for reference information and job aids on How to Change Project Options

ACTIVITY 1–4
Changing Project Options

Before You Begin
Microsoft Project Professional 2013 is open. However, you don't need to have a project file open.

Scenario
You have a few minutes at the end of your work day, so you decide to spend the time customizing your Project 2013 setup.

1. Open the **Project Options** dialog box.
   a) On the ribbon, select the **FILE** tab.
   b) On the **Backstage**, select the **Options** tab.
   Notice that the **Project Options** dialog box opens to the **General** screen.

2. Customize the ribbon.
   a) Select the **Customize Ribbon** option.
   b) Select the **New Tab** button.
   In the right column, notice that Project 2013 created **New Tab (Custom)** and **New Group (Custom)**.

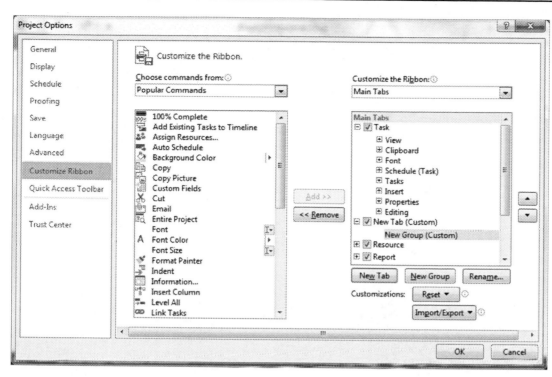

c) Select **New Tab (Custom)**, then select the **Move Up** button until **New Tab (Custom)** and **New Group (Custom)** are the top of the right column.

d) Select **New Group (Custom)**, select the first command at the top of the left column, and select the **Add** button.

Notice that Project 2013 added the selected command to **New Group (Custom)**.

e) Add the second and third commands from the left column to **New Group (Custom)**.

f) Select **OK** to close the dialog box.
Notice that the ribbon now displays a **New Tab** with a **New Group** containing three commands.

3. Customize the **Quick Access Toolbar**.

a) Reopen the **Project Options** dialog box.

b) Select the **Quick Access Toolbar** option.

c) Select the first command at the top of the left column, and select the **Add** button.
Notice that Project 2013 added the selected command to the right column.

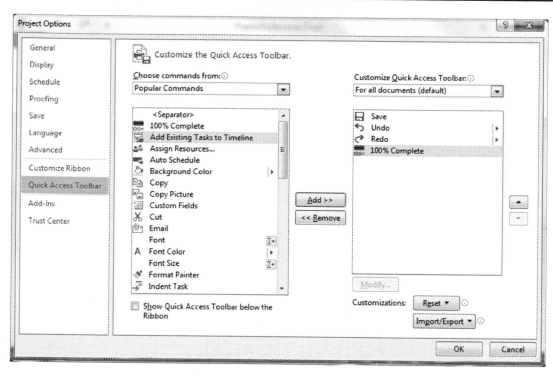

d) Select the **Redo** command in the right column, then select the **Remove** button.

Notice that Project 2013 removed the selected command from the right column.

e) Select the **Save** command at the top of the right column.

f) Select the **Move Down** button a couple of times until the **Save** command is at the bottom of the right column.

g) Select **OK** to close the dialog box.
   Notice that the **Quick Access Toolbar** displays your changes.

4. Reset the ribbon and **Quick Access Toolbar**.

   a) Reopen the **Project Options** dialog box.
   b) Select either the **Customize Ribbon** or **Quick Access Toolbar** option.
   c) Select the **Reset** button.
   d) Select the **Reset all customizations** option.
   e) In the confirmation dialog box, select **Yes**.

   f) Select **OK** to close the **Project Options** dialog box.
      Notice that both the ribbon and **Quick Access Toolbar** returned to their default states.

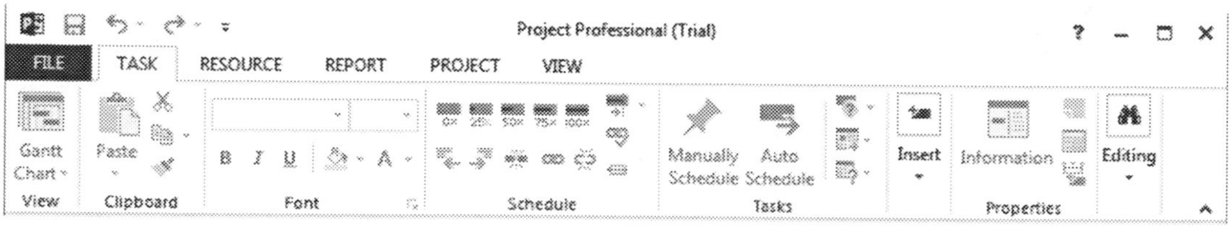

5. Close Project 2013.

TOPIC E

Extend Project with Apps

Project 2013 is packed with features. You can add even more functionality to Project 2013 by adding applications (apps) from the Office Store.

Apps for Office

You've probably had the experience of visiting an online "app store" and downloading an app to your smartphone or mobile device. The **Office Store** is the app store for the entire Microsoft Office 2013 suite—including Project 2013. It contains a number of apps, developed by third-party vendors, that enhance Project 2013. Some of the apps are free, while others must be purchased. You can access the **Office Store** (or any apps you previously installed) from the **PROJECT** tab of the ribbon by selecting the **Apps for Office** button.

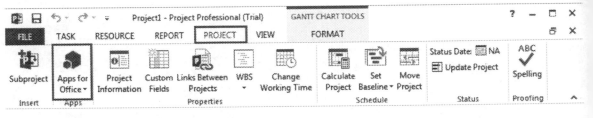

Figure 1–28: Apps for Office button.

> **Access the Checklist tile on your LogicalCHOICE course screen for reference information and job aids on How to Extend Project with Apps**

ACTIVITY 1–5
Extending Project with Apps

Before You Begin
Open Project 2013 and create a new, blank project.

Scenario
You still have a few minutes at the end of your work day, so you decide to try adding an app to Project 2013.

1. Open the **Office Store**.
   a) On the ribbon, select the **PROJECT** tab.
   b) Select the **Apps for Office** button.
   c) In the **Apps for Office** dialog box, select the **Office Store** button.

Notice that the **Office Store** opens in a web browser.

2. Choose an app from the **Office Store**.

   a) On the **Office Store** web page, scroll down to the **New Apps for Project** and **Featured App for Project** section.

New Apps for Project   more ⊕ ^

Sensei Project Dashboard™	Search The Web	Unit Converter	MindMapper	Mavenlink
★ ★ ★ ★ ★ (1)	★ ★ ★ ★ ★ (1)	★ ★ ★ ★ ★ (0)	★ ★ ★ ★ ★ (7)	★ ★ ★ ★ ★ (6)
Sensei Project Solutions	The App Refinery	MAQ LLC	RePoint Technologies	Mavenlink
Project 2013	Excel 2013, PowerPoint 2013, Project 2013, Word 2013	Excel 2013, Project 2013, Word 2013	Excel 2013, PowerPoint 2013, Project 2013, Word 2013	Excel 2013, PowerPoint 2013, Project 2013, Word 2013
$24.99	**Add**	FREE	**Add**	FREE	**Add**	$2.99	**Add**	FREE	**Add**

Featured Apps for Project

SharkPro Project View for Project Web App	TrackTimesheet Go 365	CS Milestone Trend Analysis	TPG MTA Chart	Sensei Task Analyzer
★ ★ ★ ★ ★ (0)	★ ★ ★ ★ ★ (2)	★ ★ ★ ★ ★ (1)	★ ★ ★ ★ ★ (1)	★ ★ ★ ★ ★ (0)
SharkPro Software Corporation	SOLVIN information management	Campana and Schott	TPG The Project Group	Sensei Project Solutions
	SharePoint 2013	SharePoint 2013	SharePoint 2013	Project 2013
			$29.99	**Add**	$14.99	**Add**

   b) Find a free app.

   c) Select select app icon to read more about the app.

      Normally, you would select the **Add** button to continue the process of downloading and installing the app. However, because of the limitations of the training environment, stop here.

   d) Close the browser window.

3. Close the blank project file.

Summary

In this lesson, you learned how to manage the project environment.

Will you baseline your next project? Why or why not?

What custom fields would you find useful in your project management environment?

 Note: If your instructor/organization is incorporating social media resources as part of this training, use the LogicalCHOICE Course screen to search for or begin conversations regarding this lesson.

2 Managing Task Structures

Lesson Time: 2 hours

Lesson Objectives

In this lesson, you will manage task structures. You will:

- Change a task list.
- Create a network diagram.
- Manage the critical path.
- Add lag and lead time to tasks.
- Analyze the earned value of a project.

Lesson Introduction

The commands on the **TASK** tab enable you to administer tasks—which are the building blocks of effort that need to be done to execute a project. In *Microsoft® Project 2013: Part 1,* you learned how to create and manage tasks in a new project. In this lesson, you will learn how to manage an existing task list during project execution. You will also explore network diagramming (a different way to look at task structures) and earned value (a method for monitoring how much work has been accomplished).

TOPIC A

Change a Task List

In *Microsoft® Project 2013: Part 1,* you learned how to add tasks to a project and link them together. In this topic, you'll discover how to change the tasks and task links in an existing task list.

Schedule Options

Before you try inserting a new task into an existing task list, it's a good idea to make sure that the **Autolink inserted or moved tasks** check box is checked. You can find this option by selecting **FILE** on the ribbon, selecting the **Options** tab on the **Backstage,** and selecting the **Schedule** tab in the **Project Options** dialog box.

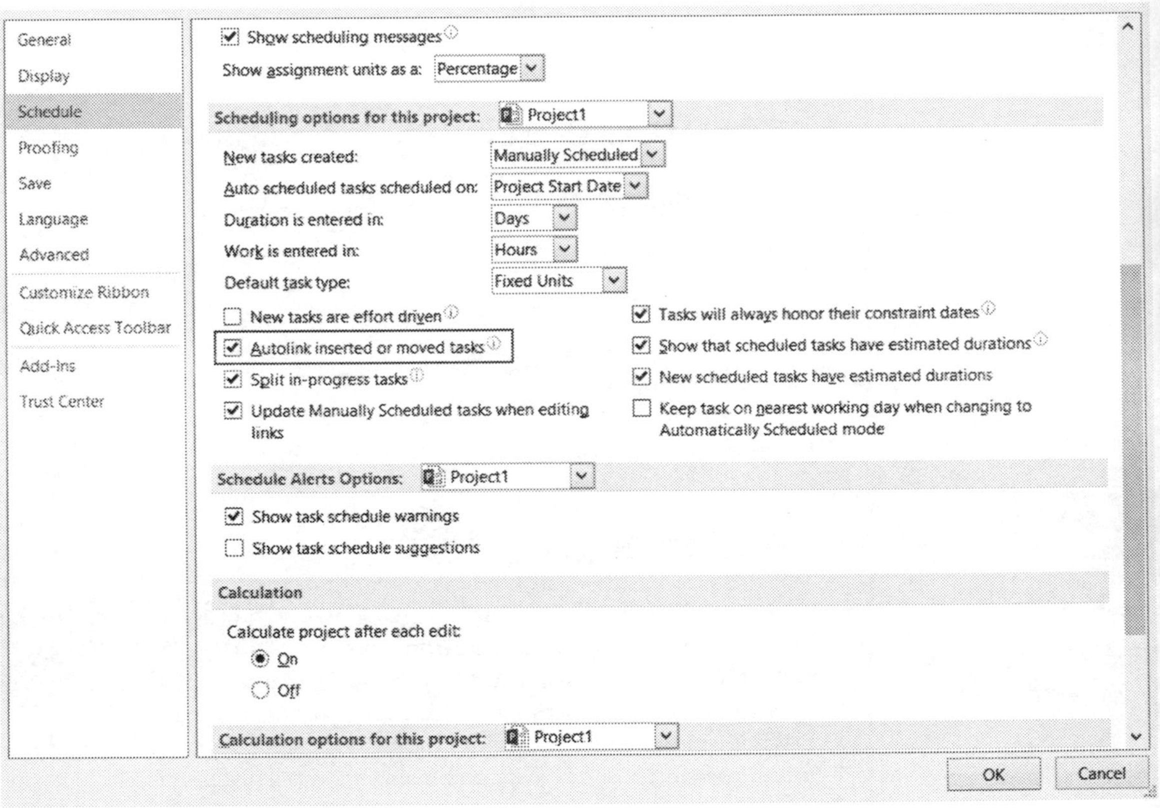

Figure 2-1: Autolink inserted or moved tasks option.

You should also make sure that the **New Tasks** option is set to **Auto Scheduled** by looking at the status bar. (You learned how to do this in *Microsoft® Project 2013: Part 1.*)

Insert Tasks

After you have verified that these options are set, go to the **Gantt Chart** view and select the task below the point where you want the new task to appear. Then, on the ribbon, select the **TASK** tab, find the **Tasks** command group, and select the **Insert Task** button. A new task will be inserted in the Gantt Chart just before the task you had selected. You can rename the new task in the **Gantt Chart** view or in the **Task Information** dialog box.

Figure 2-2: A new task inserted into an existing task list.

If the selected task was part of a *path*, the new task will be automatically inserted into the path. The selected task will become the successor of the new task, and the task that was the predecessor of the selected task will become the predecessor of the new task.

The new task will not inherit any other characteristics of the selected task. You will need to set the task duration, assign resources to it, and make any other adjustments needed.

> **Note:** Be aware that inserting a new task into an existing task structure may affect the scheduling for the entire project. Successor tasks may have to be rescheduled (automatically or manually), and the entire project may finish later than originally planned. Inserting new tasks may also increase the cost of the project.

Insert Tasks Options

There are several other ways you can use the **Insert Task** button while in the **Gantt Chart** view:

- Insert recurring tasks. For example, you might want the task **Submit status to project sponsor** to occur on a certain day each month.
- Insert blank rows. For example, you might want to separate related tasks with blank rows.
- Import tasks from Outlook®. For example, you might want to convert an Outlook task into a Microsoft® Project task.

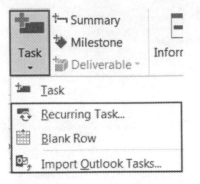

Figure 2-3: Insert Task button options.

Split Tasks

Project 2013 assumes that once an assigned resource starts a task, that person continues working on it until it is complete. In reality, however, there may be situations when a resource needs to work on a task in two or more chunks of time. This is called splitting a task. To split a task, select the **TASK** tab on the ribbon, find the **Schedule** command group, and select the **Split Task** button. Then, in the Gantt Chart, split a task bar and drag the split piece of the task bar to a new date. Project 2013 will connect the two halves of the split task bar with a dotted line.

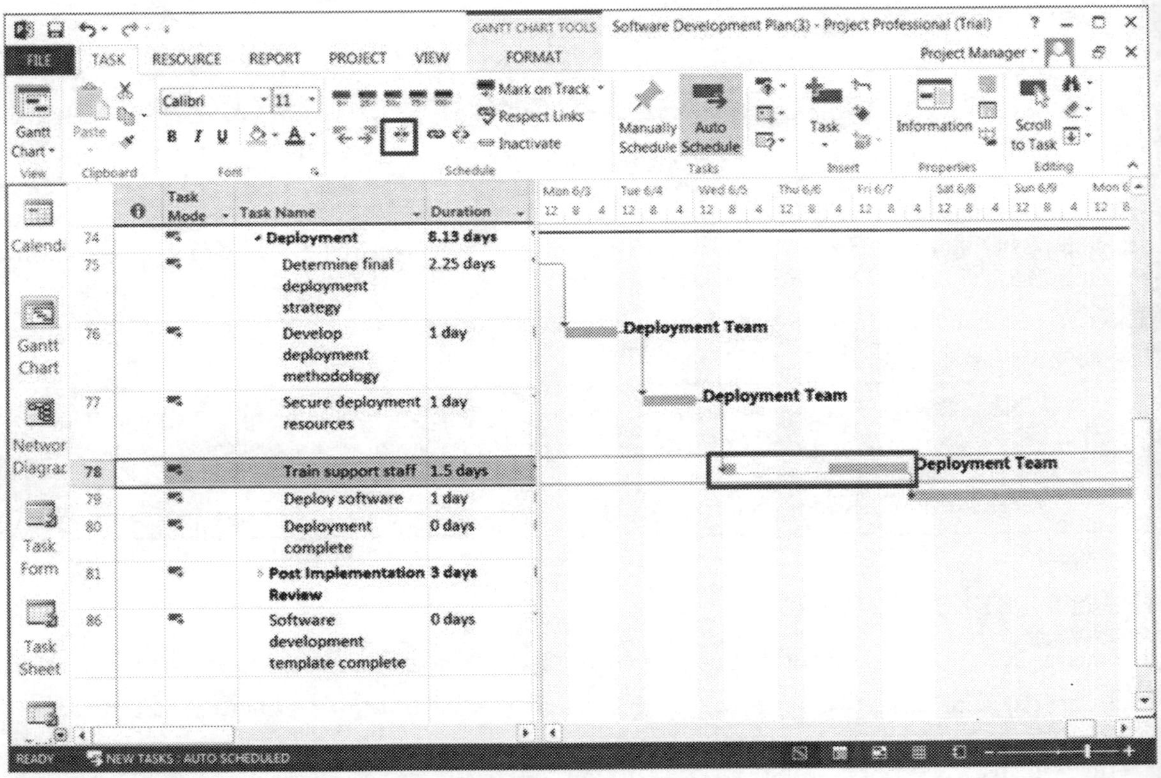

Figure 2-4: The Split Task button and a split task.

> **Note:** Be aware that splitting a task may cause the project schedule to change.

Delete Tasks

To delete an existing task from a Gantt Chart, select the entire row, right-click, and select **Delete Task.** Alternatively, you can press the **Delete** key. The entire task and all of its information will be removed from the project. If the task was part of a path, the deleted task's predecessor and successor will be linked together automatically so that the path is not broken.

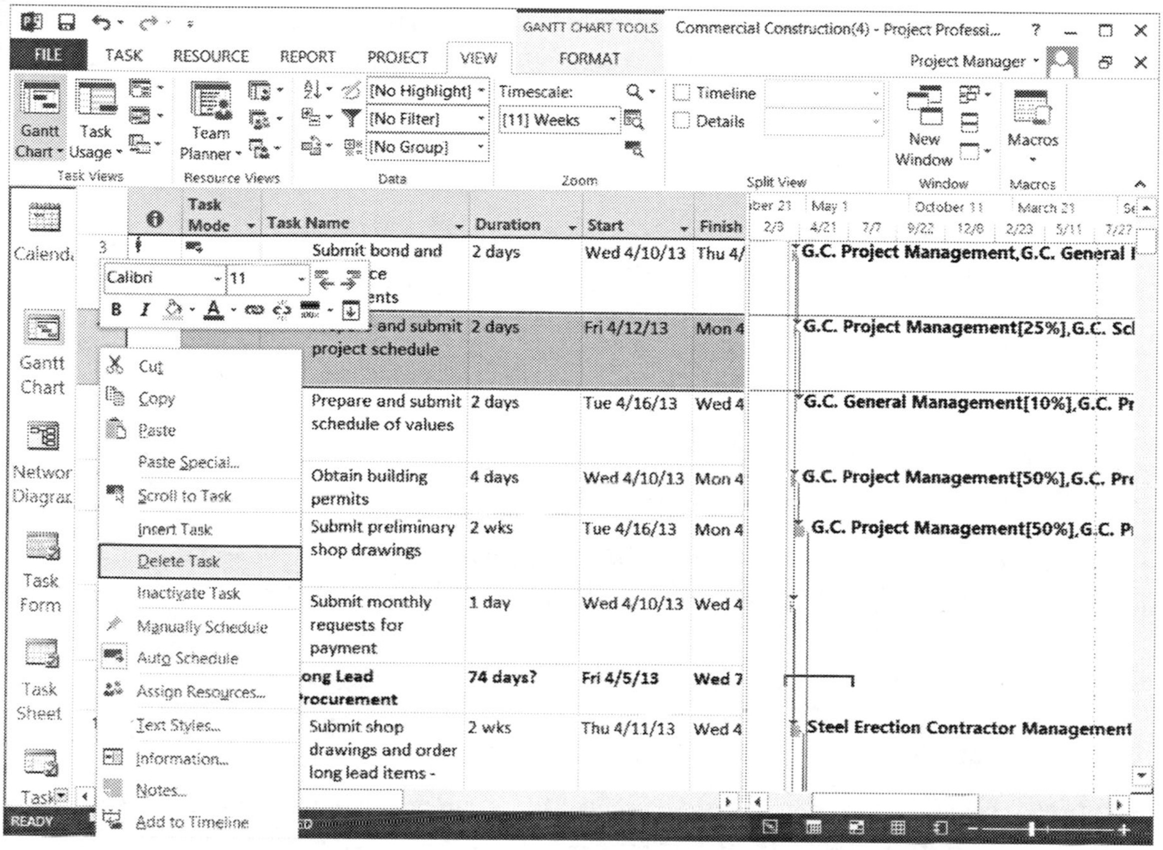

Figure 2-5: Deleting a task.

Note: Be aware that deleting a task from an existing task structure may affect the scheduling for the entire project. Successor tasks may have to be rescheduled (automatically or manually) and the entire project may finish earlier than originally planned. Deleting tasks may also decrease the cost of the project.

Move Tasks

To move an existing task in a Gantt Chart, select the entire row, and drag the row up or down to a new location.

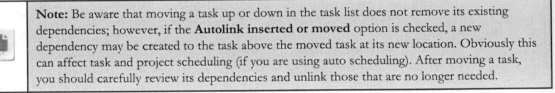

	Task Mode	Task Name	Duration	Start	Finish	Predecessors
75		⊿ Carpentry Work	15 days	Tue 9/10/13	Mon 9/30/13	
76		Install exterior sheathing and metal studs	3 wks	Tue 9/10/13	Mon 9/30/13	62,67
77		⊿ Masonry Work	110 days	Tue 6/11/13	Mon 11/11/1	
78		Rough-in plumbing at toilets and masonry walls	4 wks	Wed 8/21/13	Tue 9/17/13	74,13
79		Lay masonry at core, mechanical, and toilets	4 wks	Tue 6/11/13	Mon 7/8/13	48,49
80		Install exterior masonry work	5 wks	Tue 10/1/13	Mon 11/4/13	76
81		Install roof drains	2 days	Tue 11/5/13	Wed 11/6/13	80

Figure 2-6: Moving a task.

> **Note:** Be aware that moving a task up or down in the task list does not remove its existing dependencies; however, if the **Autolink inserted or moved** option is checked, a new dependency may be created to the task above the moved task at its new location. Obviously this can affect task and project scheduling (if you are using auto scheduling). After moving a task, you should carefully review its dependencies and unlink those that are no longer needed.

Unlink Tasks

To unlink tasks, select two or more tasks, select the **FILE** tab on the ribbon, find the **Tasks** command group, and select the **Unlink Tasks** button.

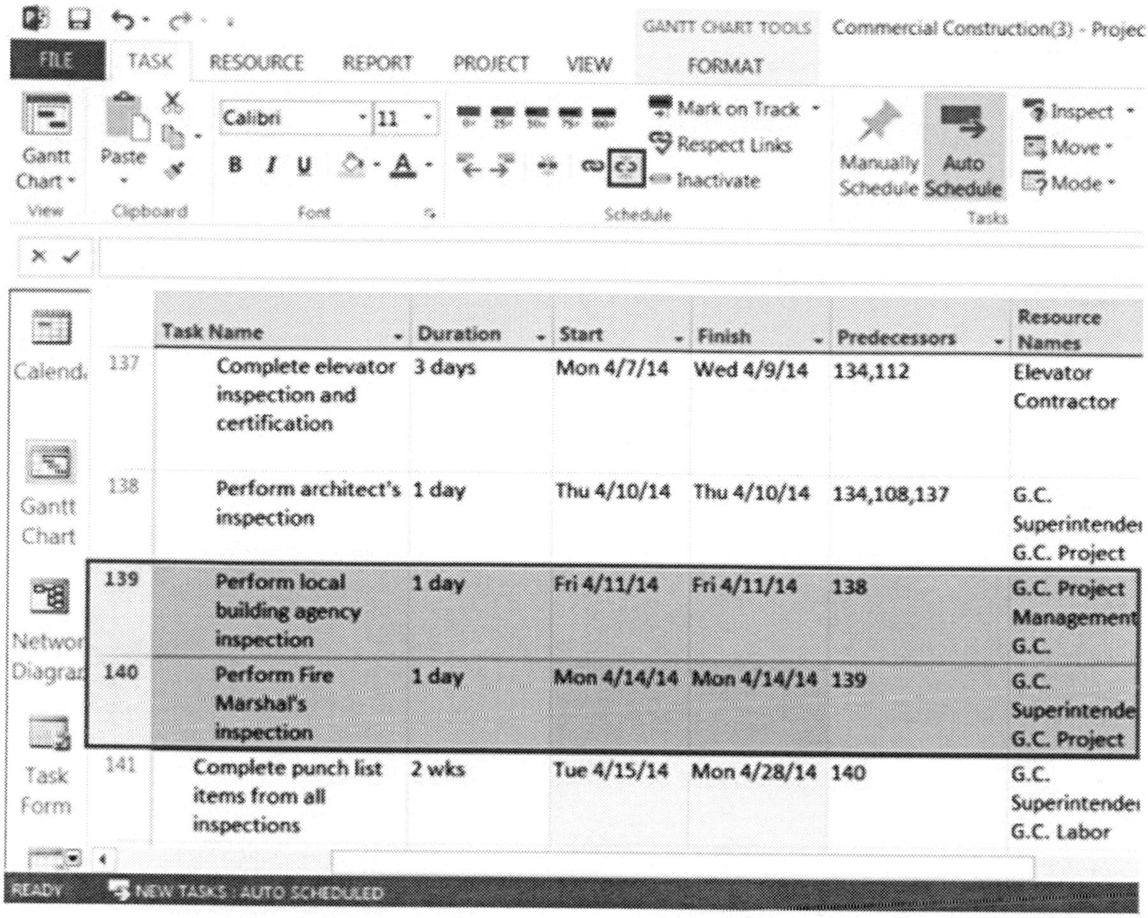

Figure 2-7: Unlinking tasks.

> **Note:** Be aware that unlinking tasks will affect scheduling of the linked tasks and may affect the scheduling of the entire project. After you unlink tasks, you should review the schedule.

Relink Tasks

Relinking tasks in an existing task list works exactly like initial linking, which you learned how to do in *Microsoft® Project 2013: Part 1.* To reiterate, select two or more tasks, select the **FILE** tab on the ribbon, find the **Tasks** command group, and select the **Link Tasks** button.

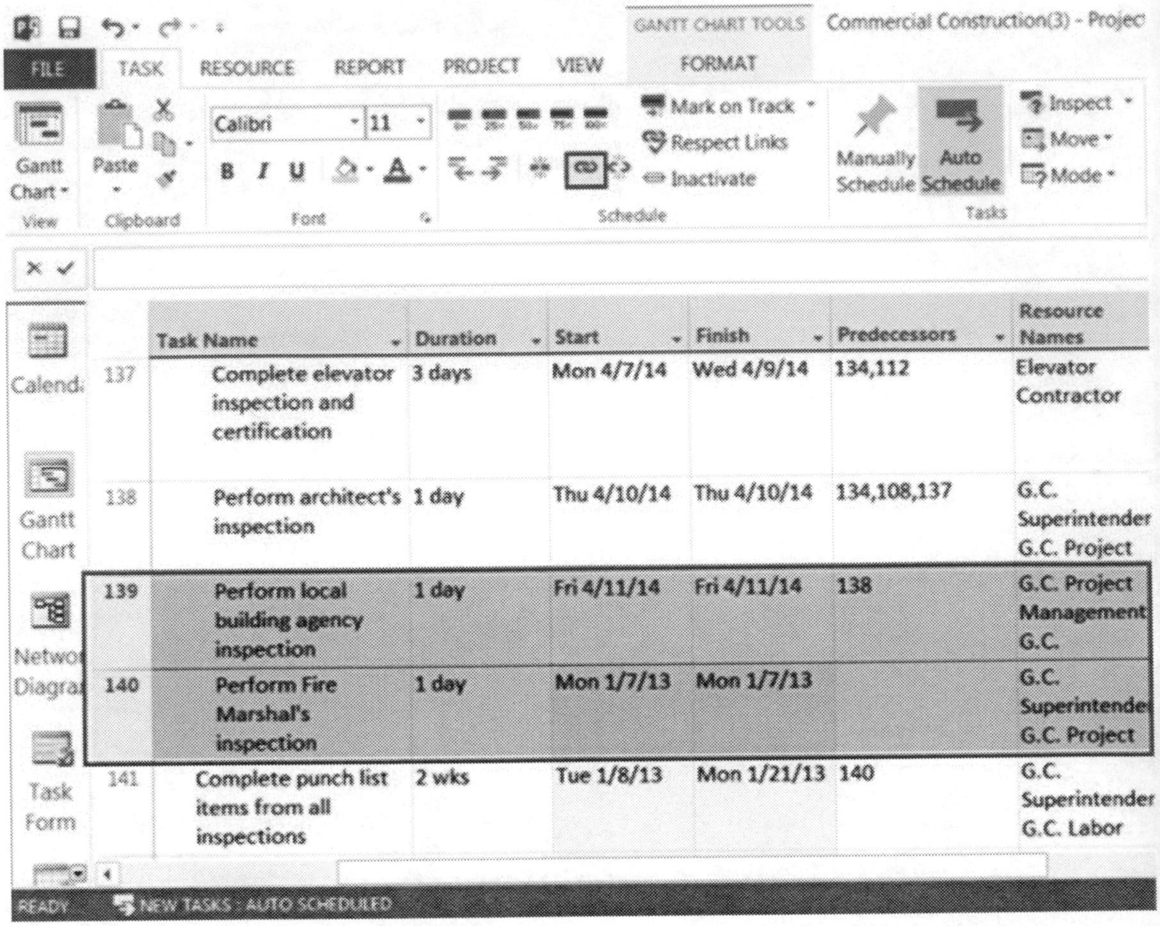

Figure 2-8: Relinking tasks.

> **Note:** Be aware that relinking tasks will affect scheduling of the linked tasks and may affect the scheduling of the entire project. After you relink tasks, you should review the schedule.

Task Inspector

As you are changing your task list, occasionally Project 2013 will underline a date in red. This indicates that there is a scheduling conflict that needs your attention. You can ask **Task Inspector** to help you identify and resolve the problem. You can open **Task Inspector** by selecting the **Inspect** button on the **TASK** tab of the ribbon. If you then select the task with the conflict, **Task Inspector** will show you the cause of the problem and suggest potential solutions.

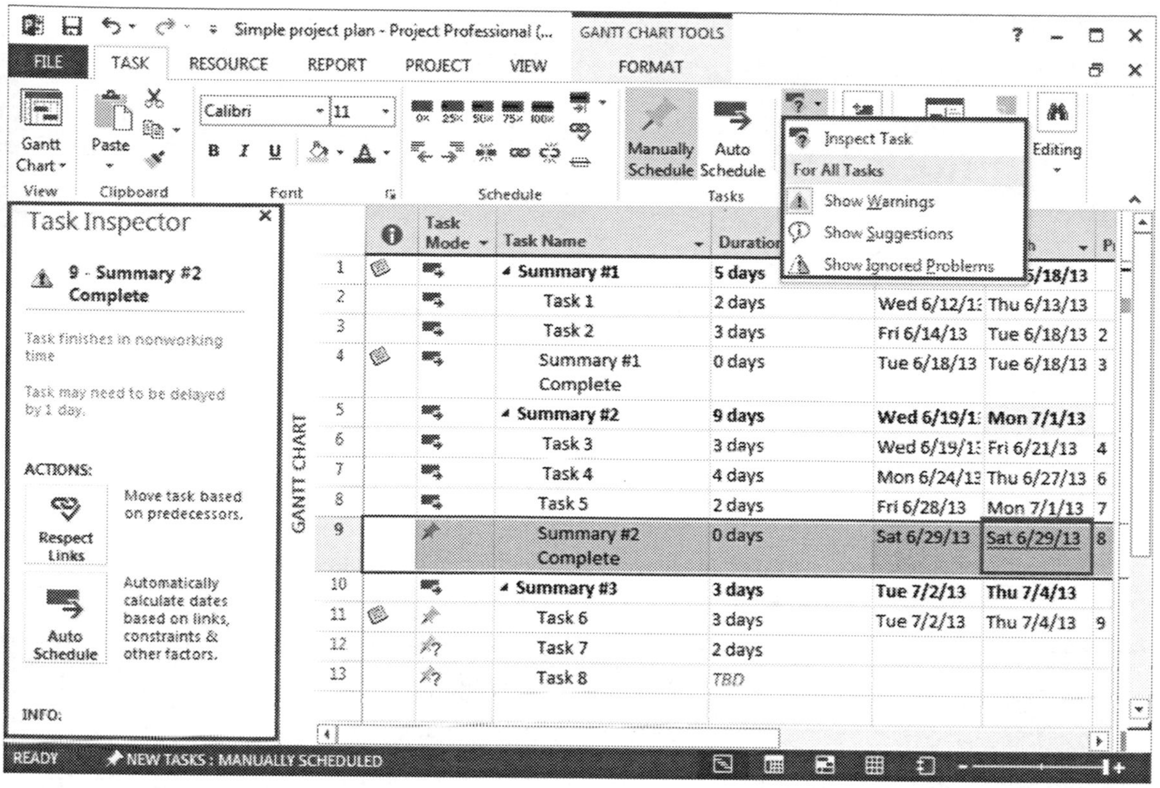

Figure 2-9: Task Inspector.

If you select the arrowhead to the right of the **Inspect** button, Project 2013 will show you a drop-down menu containing **Task Inspector** options. The **Inspect Task** option toggles **Task Inspector** on and off. The other three buttons toggle their respective features on and off in **Task Inspector**.

> **Access the Checklist tile on your LogicalCHOICE course screen for reference information and job aids on How to Change a Task List**

ACTIVITY 2-1
Changing a Task List

Data Files

C:\091111Data\Managing Task Structures\Residential Construction 2.mpp

Before You Begin

Microsoft Project Professional 2013 is open.

Scenario

You've just started the residential construction part of the GreeneCentre initiative. Your project stakeholders have requested several changes to the project plan, and your project sponsor has approved them. So, you need to update your project task list.

---

1. Open C:\091111Data\Managing Task Structures\Residential Construction 2.mpp.

2. Make sure the autolink option is active.
   a) Select the FILE tab on the ribbon.
   b) On the Backstage, select the Options tab.
   c) In the Project Options dialog box, select the Schedule tab.
   d) Scroll down to the Scheduling options for this project section.
   e) Verify that the Autolink inserted or moved tasks check box is checked.

   ✓ Autolink inserted or moved tasks ⓘ

   f) Select OK to close the Project Options dialog box.

3. Insert a new task into the task structure
   a) Make sure you are in Gantt Chart view.
   b) In the status bar, make sure the New Tasks option is set to Auto Scheduled.

   ⇥ NEW TASKS : AUTO SCHEDULED

   c) In the Gantt Chart, select row 13, Install temporary power service.
   d) If necessary, select the TASK tab on the ribbon.
   e) Find the Insert command group.
   f) Select the Insert Task button.

   Task

   g) Rename <New Task> to *Build runoff retention pond*
   h) Change the duration of the new task from 1 day? to *5 days*
      Notice that Project 2013 automatically inserted the new task into the existing path, making **Clear and grub lot** the predecessor of the new task and **Install temporary power service** the successor of the new task.

4. Split a task.

   a) In the left pane of the Gantt Chart, find row 18, **Form basement walls**.

   b) Select the **TASK** tab on the ribbon.

   c) Find the **Schedule** command group.

   d) Select the **Split Task** button.
      Notice that the mouse pointer changes its appearance to indicate that it is in task splitting mode.

   e) In the right pane of the Gantt Chart, hover the changed mouse pointer over the middle of the task bar in row 18 until the split indicator shows 2/24/15 as the **Scheduled Start** date.

   f) Click the left mouse button to split the task bar.

   g) Drag the right half of the split task bar until the split indicator shows 3/1/15 as the **Task Start** date. Notice that the two halves of the split task are connected by a dotted line.

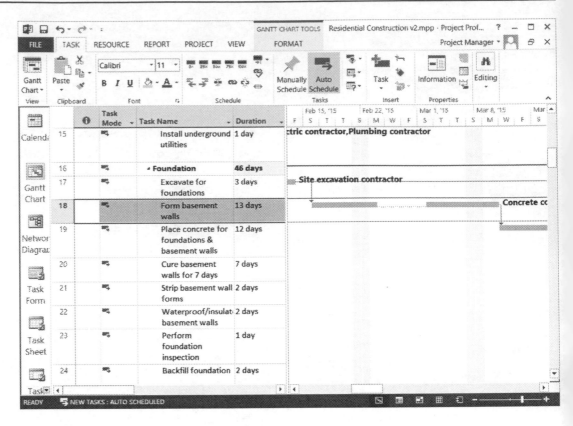

5. Delete a task.

   a) Select row 29, **Frame 1st floor corners**.

   b) Right-click and select **Delete Task**.
      Notice that Project 2013 automatically prevented a break in the path by linking **Frame 1st floor walls** and **Install 2nd floor joists**.

6. Move a task.

    a) Select row 40, **Hang 1st floor exterior doors.**
    b) If necessary, move the mouse pointer over the row number until it changes to a four-way arrow.
    c) Click and hold the left mouse button.
    d) Move the row between row 36, **Install 1st floor sheathing**, and row 37, **Install 2nd floor sheathing.**
    e) Release the left mouse button.
    Notice that Project 2013 did not change the path.

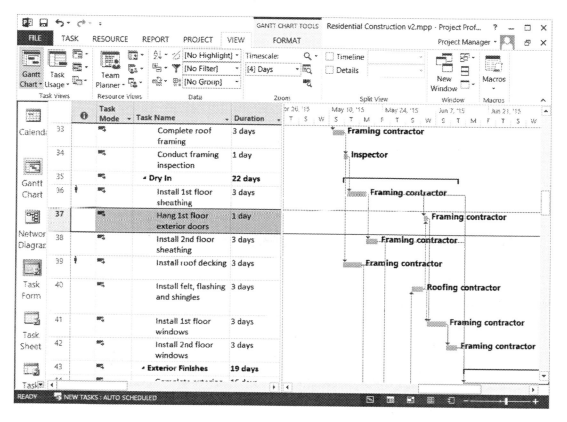

7. Unlink a task.

    a) Select row 106, **Cleanup for occupancy.**
    b) If necessary, select the **TASK** tab on the ribbon.
    c) Find the **Schedule** command group.

    d) Select the **Unlink Tasks** button.
    Notice that the **Predecessors** in rows 106 and 107 disappeared and the **Start** and **Finish** dates for several tasks were affected.

8. Relink a task.

   a) Select rows 105, 106, and 107.

   b) If necessary, select the **TASK** tab on the ribbon.

   c) Find the **Schedule** command group.

   d) Select the **Link Tasks** button.
      Notice that the **Predecessors** in rows 106 and 107 appeared and the **Start** and **Finish** dates for several tasks were affected.

9. Save the file in C:\091111Data\Managing Task Structures as *My Residential Construction 2.mpp* and then close the file.

TOPIC B

Create a Network Diagram

Up to now, you have mainly looked at projects though the lens of the Gantt Chart—which is the most well-known way to illustrate project information. However, every project manager should be familiar with another important method for illustrating project information—the network diagram. In this section, you will explore network diagramming.

Network Diagramming

Network diagramming (also called Precedence Diagramming Method or PDM) is a method for illustrating project information that emphasizes task sequencing and dependencies among tasks. In this methodology, tasks are depicted as boxes (known as nodes), and dependencies are depicted as arrows connecting the nodes.

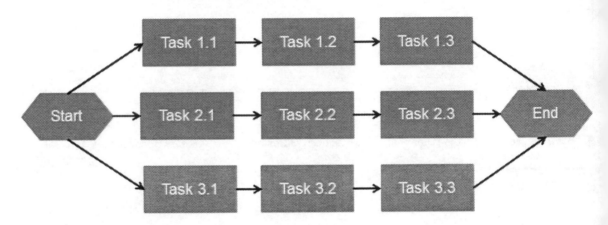

Figure 2-10: A network diagram.

A network diagram is especially useful when you need to pay more attention to task sequencing rather than task scheduling.

> **Note:** PDM was developed in the early 1960s by H.B. Zachry Company in cooperation with IBM.

Network Diagram View

Whenever you add tasks to a Gantt Chart and link them together, Project 2013 is creating a network diagram behind the scenes. To see it, select the **Network Diagram** button on the **View Bar**.

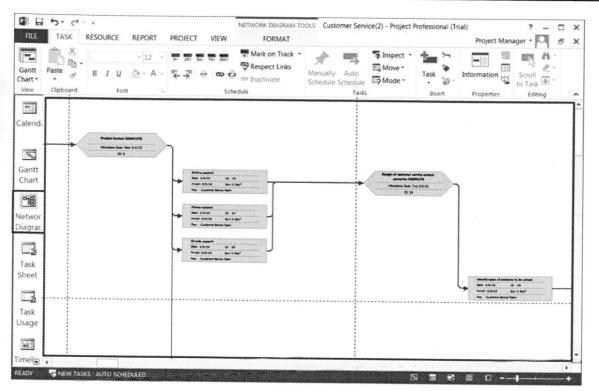

Figure 2-11: Network Diagram view.

Task Nodes

You can also use the **Network Diagram** view to construct your initial project plan. To start building a project plan, open a blank project, select the **Network Diagram** view, and select the **Insert Task** button on the **TASK** tab on the ribbon. A node will appear representing the new task.

\<New Task\>	
Start: 1/7/13	ID: 1
Finish: 1/7/13	Dur: 1 day?
Res:	

Figure 2-12: Node representing a task.

Node Task Fields

The node displays six task fields:

- **Name** of the task, which initially will be blank or have a **\<New Task\>** placeholder. You can type a desired task name directly into this field.
- **Start** date of the task, which will initially be the computer's current date.
- **ID** number of the task, which is automatically assigned by Project 2013.
- **Finish** date of the task, which will be the **Start** date plus the **Duration**.
- **Duration** of the task, which will initially be 1 day (estimated). You can type a different duration directly into this field.
- **Resource Names** assigned to the task, which initially will be vacant. You can type resource names directly into this field.

Add Nodes and Links

You can continue building your new project plan by adding additional nodes and links to the network diagram. To add a new node and link, select the first node, press and hold the left mouse button, drag the mouse pointer to the right of the node, and release.

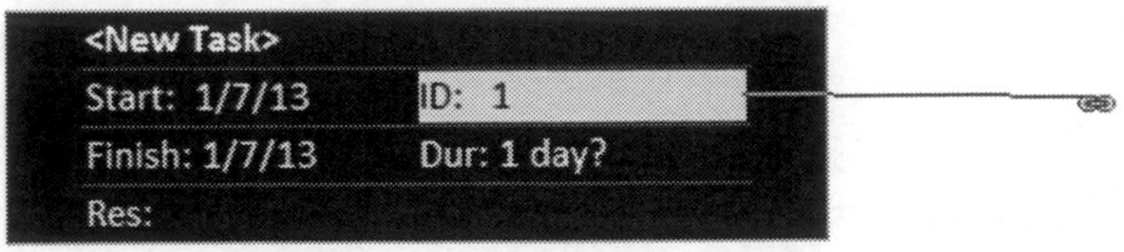

Figure 2–13: Adding a node and link.

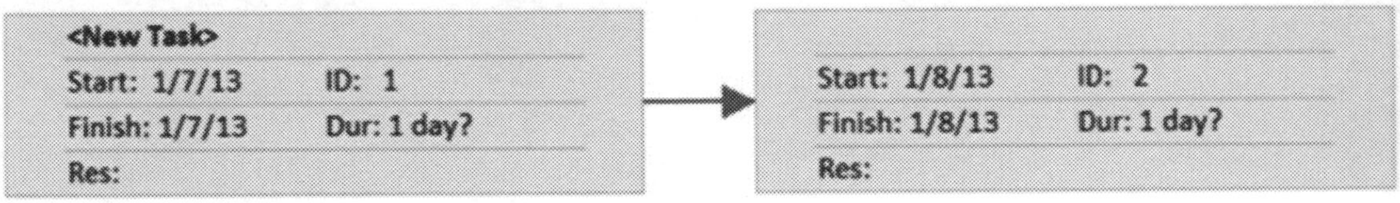

Figure 2–14: Node and link added.

Milestones and Summary Nodes

In **Network Diagram** view, milestone nodes are shown as hexagons, and summary nodes are shown as parallelograms.

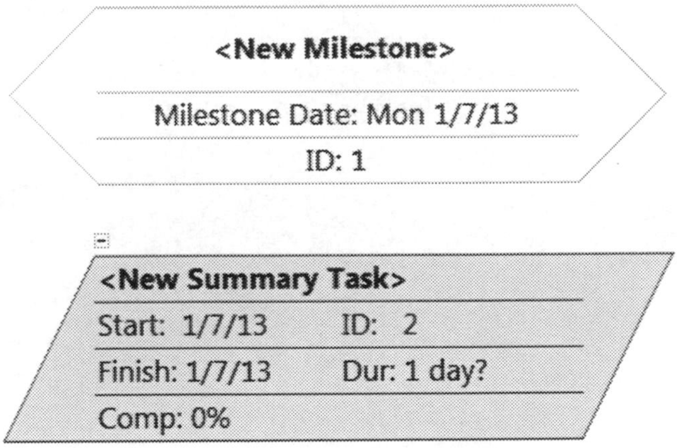

Figure 2–15: Milestone and summary task nodes.

Paths

A path is a chain of linked tasks from a starting point to an ending point. Simple projects may have a single path, while complex projects can have multiple paths that run in parallel—diverging and converging.

* **Path 1** ⟶
* **Path 2** ┄┄>
* **Path 3** – →

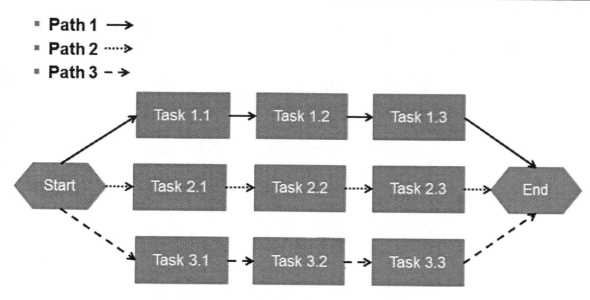

Figure 2-16: Multiple paths.

Access the Checklist tile on your LogicalCHOICE course screen for reference information and job aids on How to Create a Network Diagram

ACTIVITY 2–2
Creating a Network Diagram

Before You Begin
Microsoft Project Professional 2013 is open.

Scenario
Sylvia Deaton, your project sponsor, has asked you to create a high-level network diagram for a new project—marketing the GreeneCentre initiative to potential commercial and residential customers. Here are the tasks Sylvia would like you to include:

Task	Duration (Days)
Start Marketing Project	0
Review Business Strategy Landscape	25
Develop Campaign Concepts	50
Develop Prototype Campaign Materials	20
Prototype Campaign Materials Complete	0
Test and Revise Campaign Materials	30
Produce Campaign Materials	15
Launch Campaign	0
Run Campaign	50
Evaluate Campaign Effectiveness	5
End Marketing Project	0

Sylvia says that this project will start April 1, 2015. She says that all of the tasks are in a single path, and the tasks with zero duration are milestones.

---

1. Create a new blank project file.

2. On the **View Bar,** select the **Network Diagram** button.

3. Create the first milestone node.
   a) In the **Network Diagram** view, move the mouse pointer to the upper-left corner of the large empty pane.
   b) Click and hold the left mouse button. The mouse pointer will change appearance.
   c) Drag the mouse pointer diagonally to trace a rectangle.
   d) Release the left mouse button.
   Notice that a rectangular node appears.
   e) In the top cell of the node, type *Start Marketing Project*
   f) In the **Start** cell of the node, type *4/1/15*
   g) In the **Dur** (Duration) cell of the node, type *0*
   Notice that the node changes from a rectangle to a hexagon to indicate that it is a milestone.

Start Marketing Project

Milestone Date: 4/1/15

ID: 1

4. Create the first task node.

   a) Move the mouse pointer over the milestone you created in the previous step.
   b) Click and hold the left mouse button.
   c) Drag the mouse pointer outside the milestone toward the right. The mouse pointer will change appearance.
   d) Release the left mouse button.
      Notice that a new rectangular node appears.
   e) In the top cell of the new node, type *Review Business Strategy Landscape*
   f) In the **Dur** cell of the new node, type *25*

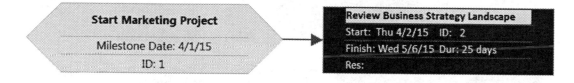

5. Add the remaining task and milestone nodes to the network.
   When you are done, you should have a network diagram with 11 linked nodes. Four of the nodes should be milestones (represented by hexagons) and seven of the nodes should be tasks (represented by rectangles).

6. Save the file in C:\091111Data\Managing Task Structures as *My GreeneCentre Marketing Campaign.mpp* and then close the file.

TOPIC C

Manage the Critical Path

Every task is important, but those tasks that directly determine the total duration of the project are especially critical. In this topic we will discuss the importance of your project's critical path.

Critical Path

The *critical path* is the longest path in a project, calculated by summing the durations of the individual tasks in the path, that determines the duration of the project.

In other words, the project duration cannot be shorter than the total duration of the tasks in the critical path. Generally, a project has a single critical path, but may have more than one.

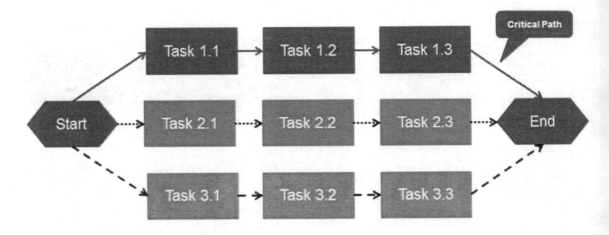

Figure 2-17: The critical path.

Pay Attention to the Critical Path

It is essential that you manage the critical path. If one or more tasks on the critical path falls behind schedule, then the entire project will take longer than planned. That could mean missing important deadlines or spending more money than budgeted.

 Note: To further explore the importance of the critical path, you can access the LearnTO **Manage the Critical Path** presentation from the **LearnTO** tile on the LogicalCHOICE Course screen.

View the Critical Path

Project 2013 automatically calculates the critical path for you. In both the **Gantt Chart** and **Network Diagram** views, tasks on the critical path are depicted in red.

Network Diagram

Gantt Chart

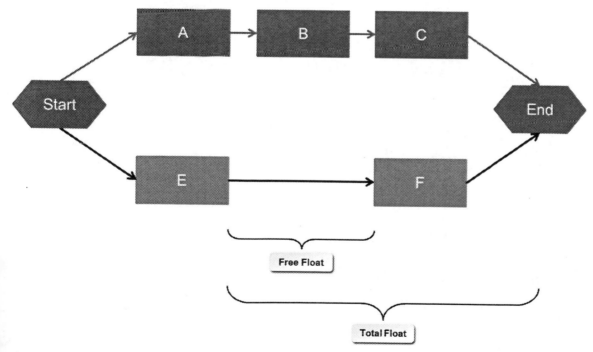

Figure 2-18: The critical path in a network diagram.

 Note: If the critical path is not showing up as red in your version of Project 2013, you probably need to change a setting. Select the **FORMAT** tab on the ribbon, find the **Bar Styles** command group, and check the **Critical Tasks** check box.

Float (Slack)

Float (also known as slack) is the amount of time that a task can be delayed without affecting it's successors (free float) or the project completion date (total float). A task on the critical path has zero free float.

Figure 2-19: Float (Slack)

You can see task float by selecting the **VIEW** tab of the ribbon, finding the **Data** command group, selecting the **Tables** button drop-down menu, and selecting the **Schedule** table. This table includes **Free Slack** and **Total Slack** columns.

 Access the Checklist tile on your LogicalCHOICE course screen for reference information and job aids on How to View the Critical Path

ACTIVITY 2-3
Managing the Critical Path

Before You Begin
Microsoft® Project Professional 2013 is open.

Data Files
C:\091111Data\Managing Task Structures\My Residential Construction 2.mpp

Scenario
You recently started the residential construction project of the GreeneCentre initiative. The project stakeholders set Monday, August 17, 2015, as the project completion date. This date will be listed in sales materials targeted at prospective residents. You want to identify and pay special attention to the tasks on the critical path to ensure that the project deadline is achieved.

---

1. Reopen C:\091111Data\Managing Task Structures\My Residential Construction 2.mpp.

2. Examine the critical path in the **Network Diagram** view.
   a) In the **View Bar**, select the **Network Diagram** option.
   b) In the view, scroll vertically and horizontally to find tasks 84, 86, 87, and 89.

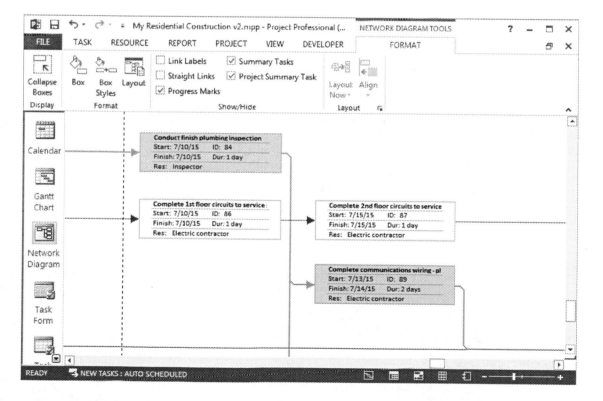

3. Answer the following question.

   Which tasks above have zero total slack? (Select two.)
   ☐ Conduct finish plumbing inspection

☐ Complete 1st floor circuits to service panel

☐ Complete 2nd floor circuits to service panel

☐ Complete communications wiring - phone, cable, computer, alarm

4. Examine the critical path in the **Gantt Chart** view.

a) In the **View Bar**, select the **Gantt Chart** option.

b) In the ribbon, select the **GANTT CHART TOOLS FORMAT** contextual tab.

c) Find the **Bar Styles** command group.

d) Make sure the **Critical Tasks** box is checked. If it is not checked, check it.

e) In the right pane of the view, scroll vertically and horizontally to find bars and arrows in red.

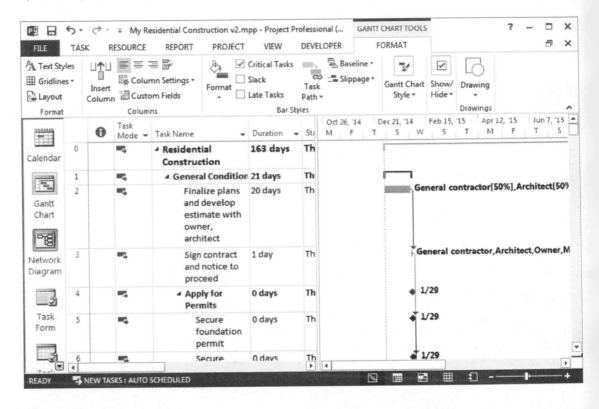

5. True or False? If the task Finalize plans and develop estimate with owner, architect takes longer than 20 days to complete, the project will still finish on time.

☐ True

☐ False

6. Save and close the file.

TOPIC D

Use Lag and Lead

As you may recall from *Microsoft® Project 2013: Part 1,* whenever two tasks are linked, the default is to create a Finish-to-Start (FS) dependency. Project 2013 assumes that as soon as the first task finishes, the second task starts immediately. However, there may be situations when you need there to be a delay or overlap between two linked tasks. In this topic, you will discuss the concepts of lag and lead.

Lag

Normally in a Finish-to-Start (FS) relationship, there is no delay or overlap between the end of Task A and the beginning of Task B.

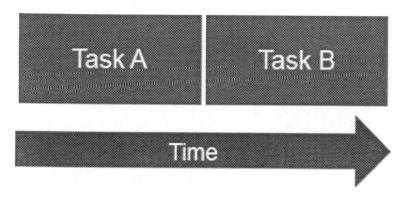

Figure 2-20: Normal Finish-to-Start relationship.

Lag is a delay in time between two tasks that are linked together. For example, in the following figure, even though Task A and Task B have an FS relationship, Task B is scheduled to begin some time after Task A is completed rather than immediately.

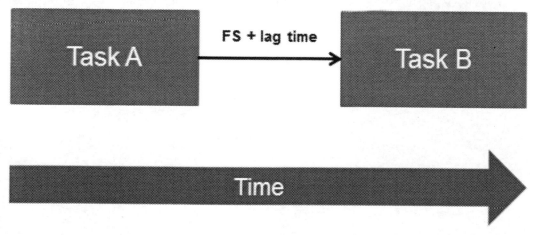

Figure 2-21: Lag.

Here's a simple example to help you understand lag. Pretend you are making a birthday cake. You must bake the cake before you can put frosting on the cake. So, there is an FS relationship between baking the cake and frosting the cake. However, after you bake the cake, you must wait until the cake has cooled down before you can apply the frosting. The delay period is the lag time.

Add Lag

You can add lag to a link by opening the **Task Information** dialog box of the successor task, selecting the **Predecessors** tab, and typing a positive value into the **Lag** column.

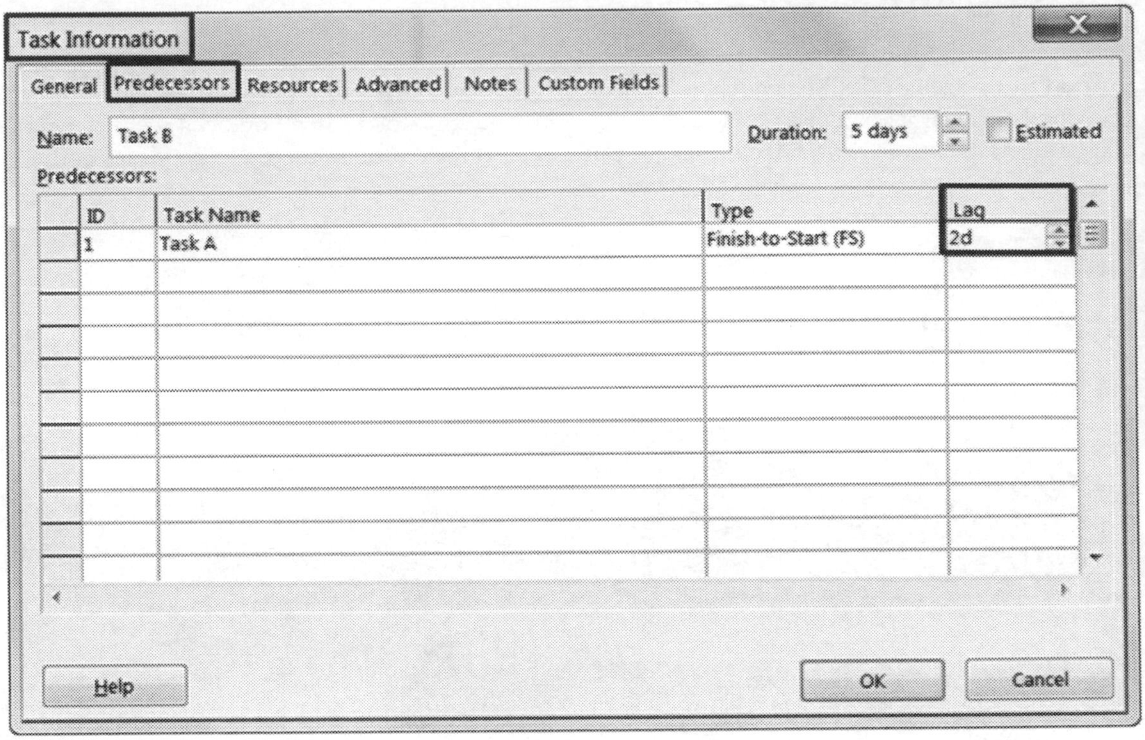

Figure 2-22: Entering lag.

Lead

Lead is an overlap in time between two tasks that are linked together. For example, in the following figure, even though Task A and Task B have an FS relationship, Task B is scheduled to begin when Task A is only about 50 percent complete rather than 100 percent complete.

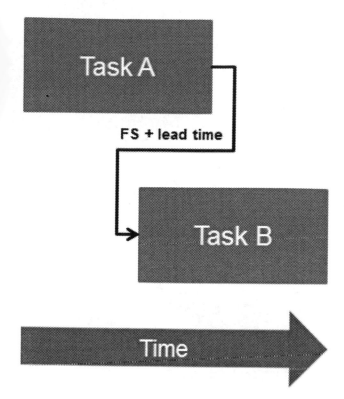

Figure 2-23: Lead.

Here's a simple example to help you understand lead. Let's return to the birthday cake scenario. You must mix the cake's ingredients before you bake the cake in the oven. So, there is an FS relationship between mixing the cake and baking the cake. However, you want the oven to preheat while you are mixing the cake so that the oven will be at the proper temperature for baking when you have finished mixing the cake. The preheating period is the lead time.

Add Lead

You can add lead to a link by opening the **Task Information** dialog box of the successor task, selecting the **Predecessors** tab, and typing a negative value into the **Lag** column. (In other words, negative lag is lead.)

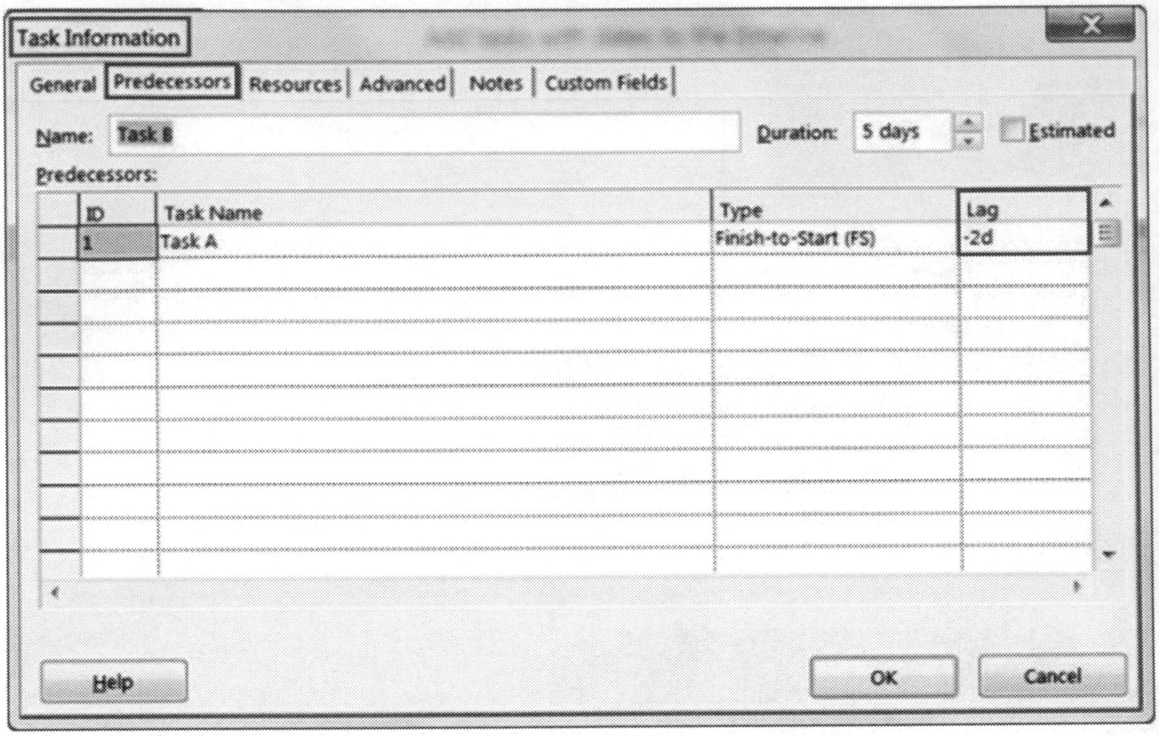

Figure 2–24: Entering lead.

Access the Checklist tile on your LogicalCHOICE course screen for reference information and job aids on How to Add Lag and Lead Time to Linked Tasks

ACTIVITY 2-4
Adding Lag and Lead Time

Data Files

C:\091111Data\Managing Task Structures\Commercial Construction 2.mpp

Before You Begin

Microsoft Project Professional 2013 is open.

Scenario

While talking to the general contractor of the commercial construction part of the GreeneCentre initiative, you learn that some of the linked tasks in the project plan can actually overlap in time. You also learn that other linked tasks actually require delay time between them. You decide to add lead and lag time to these tasks.

---

1. Open C:\091111Data\Managing Task Structures\Commercial Construction 2.mpp.

2. Add lag time to linked tasks.
   a) Scroll down the Gantt Chart to row 35.
   b) Double-click **Rough-in electric and plumbing in elevator.**
   c) In the **Task Information** dialog box, select the **Predecessors** tab.
   d) In the **Lag** column, change 0d to *2d*
   e) Select **OK** to close the dialog box.
      In the Gantt Chart, notice that the **Predecessors** cell of the task now reads **33FS+2 days** to show the lag time between the task and its predecessor. Also notice that the **Start** and **Finish** dates of several successor tasks have changed.

3. Add lead time to linked tasks.

   a) Scroll down the Gantt Chart to row 95.

   b) Double-click **Install interior doors and hardware**.

   c) In the **Task Information** dialog box, select the **Predecessors** tab.

   d) In the **Lag** column, change 0d to *-5d*

   e) Select **OK** to close the dialog box.
   In the Gantt Chart, notice that the **Predecessors** cell of the task now reads **94FS-5 days** to show the lead time between the task and its predecessor. Also notice that the **Start** and **Finish** dates of several successor tasks have changed.

4. Save the file in C:\091111Data\Managing Task Structures as *My Commercial Construction 2.mpp* and then close the file.

TOPIC E

Analyze Earned Value

As your project is being executed, it is vital that you monitor scope completed, time elapsed, and cost spent on the project to make sure that your project will be completed according to specifications, on time, and within budget. Earned value is a powerful tool for monitoring scope, time, and cost. Earned value is a simple concept that has a reputation for being complicated. In this topic, you will explore the concept of earned value and how to use it.

Earned Value

Earned value (EV) is the budgeted cost of work performed (BCWP) as of a specific status date. In other words, earned value asks the question, "Given the amount of work done so far on the project, how much money should we have spent?" The earned value is then compared to the planned value (PV) (also known as the budgeted cost of work scheduled [BCWS]) and the actual cost (AC) (also known as the actual cost of work performed [ACWP]) to determine the project's status. If the PV is higher than the EV, then the project is behind schedule. If the AC is higher than the EV, then the project is over budget.

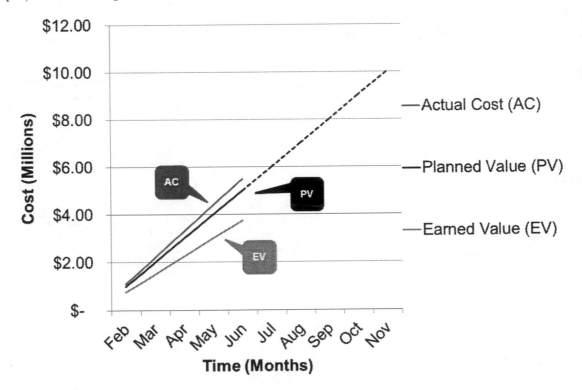

Figure 2-25: An example of earned value.

Here's an example to help you understand earned value and its usefulness: Matt Coldwell works for a renewable energy company that installs commercial-grade wind turbines. The company has a contract to deploy 10 turbines within 10 months at a cost of $10 million. According to Matt's project plan, one turbine will be deployed every month at a cost of $1 million per month. It is now five months into the project. At this point in time the EV is $3.75 million, the PV is $5 million, and the AC is $5.5 million. Because the PV is higher than the EV, the project is behind schedule. Because the AC is higher than the EV, the project is over budget. Matt's project is in serious trouble! He should take immediate corrective action to get it back on track.

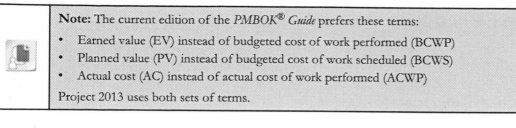

Note: The current edition of the *PMBOK® Guide* prefers these terms:

- Earned value (EV) instead of budgeted cost of work performed (BCWP)
- Planned value (PV) instead of budgeted cost of work scheduled (BCWS)
- Actual cost (AC) instead of actual cost of work performed (ACWP)

Project 2013 uses both sets of terms.

Earned Value Methods

Project 2013 has two methods for calculating earned value—**% Complete** and **Physical % Complete**. What's the difference?

% Complete is the percentage of actual time spent on a task or project versus planned time. For example, if a task is scheduled to be 40 hours in duration and 20 hours have been spent so far, the task is 50% complete.

20 hours out of 40 hours

Figure 2–26: % Complete.

Physical % Complete is the percentage of actual output completed on a task or project versus planned output. For example, if a task is to produce 100 widgets and 40 widgets have been produced, the task is 40% physically complete.

40 widgets out of 100 widgets

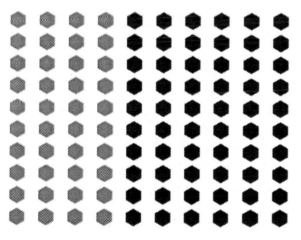

Figure 2–27: Physical % Complete.

% Complete vs. Physical % Complete

By default, Project 2013 uses **% Complete** to calculate earned value. This is the best method to use when most of the resources for the project are people costed by the hour. However, if most of the resources for the project are materials costed by the unit, it is better to use **Physical % Complete.**

Change Earned Value Method

You can change the earned value method for an entire project using the **Advanced** tab of the **Project Options** dialog box. (A reminder that you can open the **Project Options** dialog box by selecting **FILE** on the ribbon and then selecting the **Options** tab on the **Backstage.**)

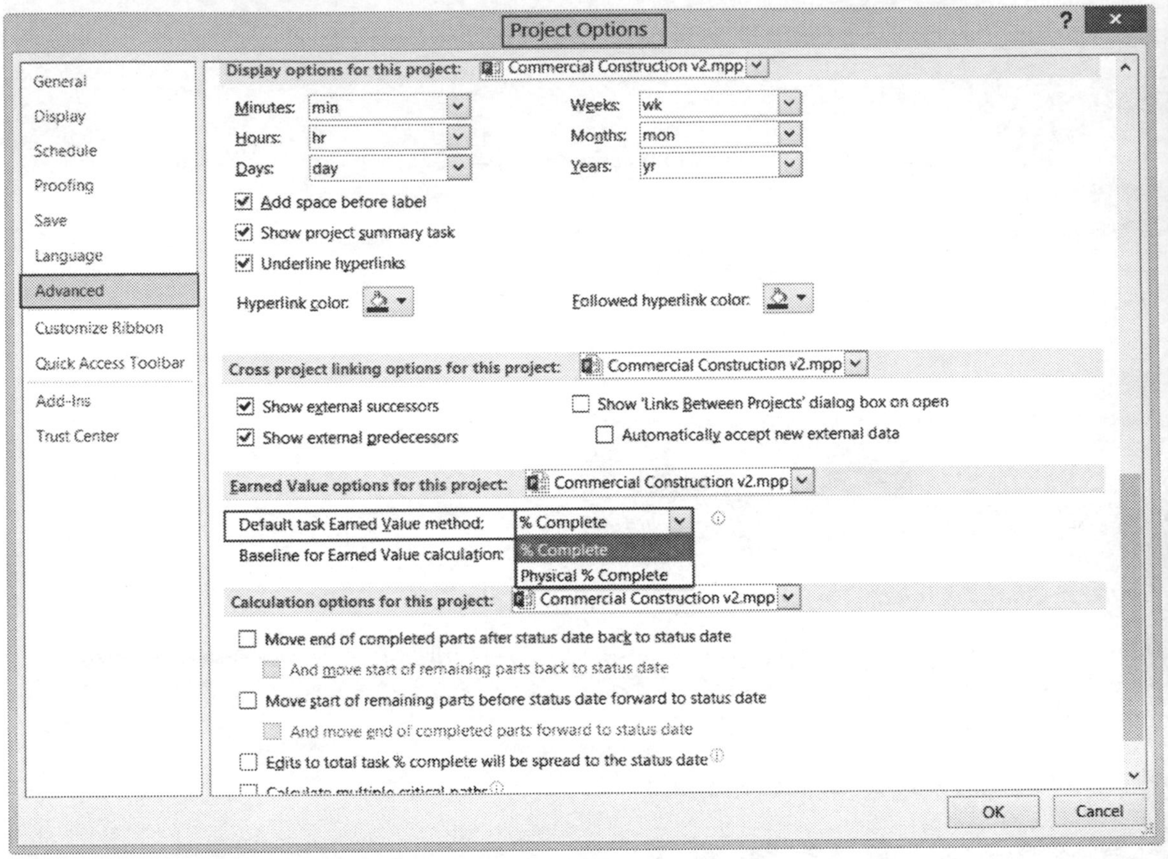

Figure 2-28: Changing a project's earned value method.

You can also change the earned value method for an individual task on the **Advanced** tab of the **Task Information** dialog box.

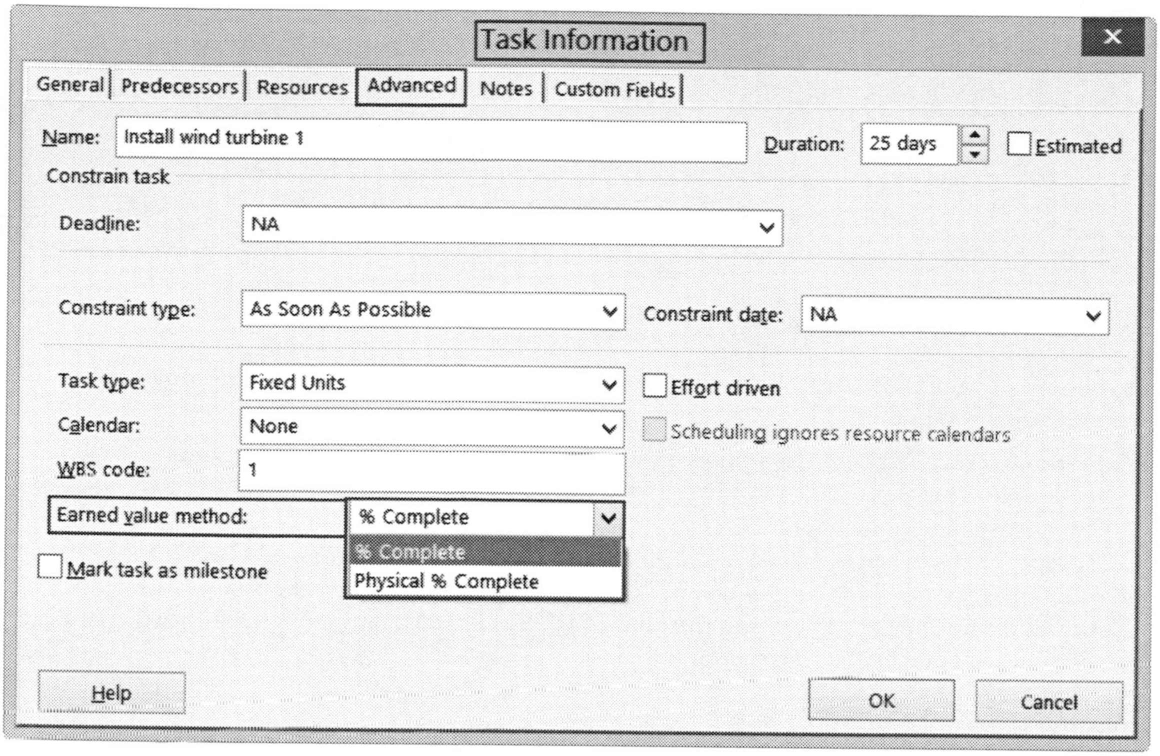

Figure 2-29: Changing a task's earned value method.

Prepare to Use Earned Value

Before you can actually use the earned value analysis tools in Project 2013, you must prepare the project:

- Input rates for each resource. You learned how to do this in *Microsoft® Project 2013: Part 1*.
- Set the project baseline. You learned how to do this earlier in this course.
- Set the project status date. You can do this with the **Status Date** button.
- Update the status of project tasks. You can do this with the **Mark on Track** button.

Set Status Date

You will find the **Status Date** button on the **PROJECT** tab of the ribbon, in the **Status** command group. Set the status date to the date you would like to see the project's earned value.

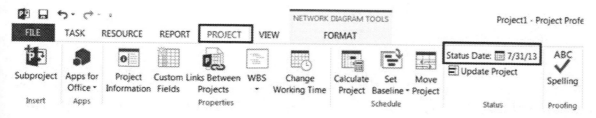

Figure 2-30: Status Date button.

Mark on Track and Update Tasks

You will find the **Mark on Track** button on the **TASK** tab of the ribbon, in the **Schedule** command group.

Figure 2-31: Mark on Track button.

If you select one or more tasks in a view, and then select the **Mark on Track** drop-down arrow, you will be shown two options:

- **Mark on Track.** Choose this option if the selected task is exactly where it should be as of the status date. That is, the task actually started and ended when planned, and its actual duration was the same as the planned duration.

- **Update Tasks.** Choose this option if the task is not exactly where it should be as of the status date. The **Update Tasks** dialog box will open in which you can enter the **% Complete,** the **Actual duration,** the **Remaining duration,** the **Actual Start,** and the **Actual Finish.** You can add notes about why the task is not on track.

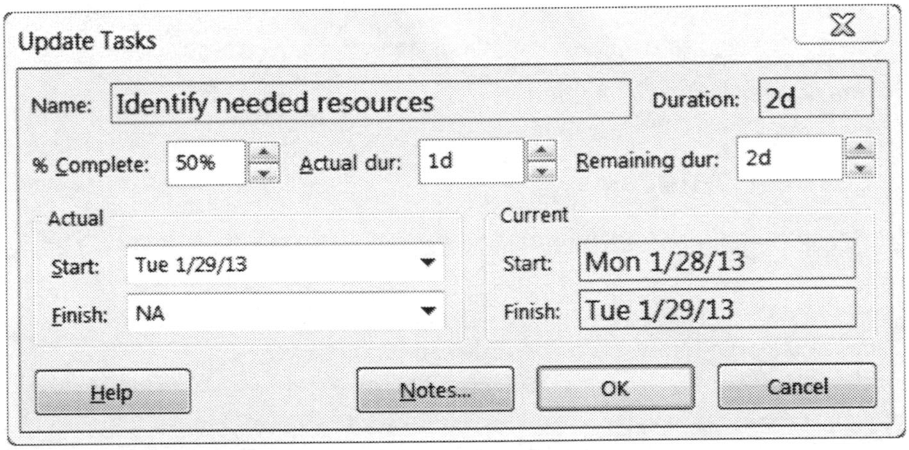

Figure 2-32: Update Tasks dialog box.

> **Note:** You can only select **Mark on Track** for tasks that are scheduled to be complete on or before the status date.

Percent Complete

To quickly update the status of a task, you can use the percent complete buttons in the **Schedule** command group of the **TASK** tab. Select one or more tasks, and then select a button that corresponds to the percentage of the task's duration that has been completed. For example, if a task is scheduled to take two days to complete and the task has been underway for one day, you would mark the task as 50% complete.

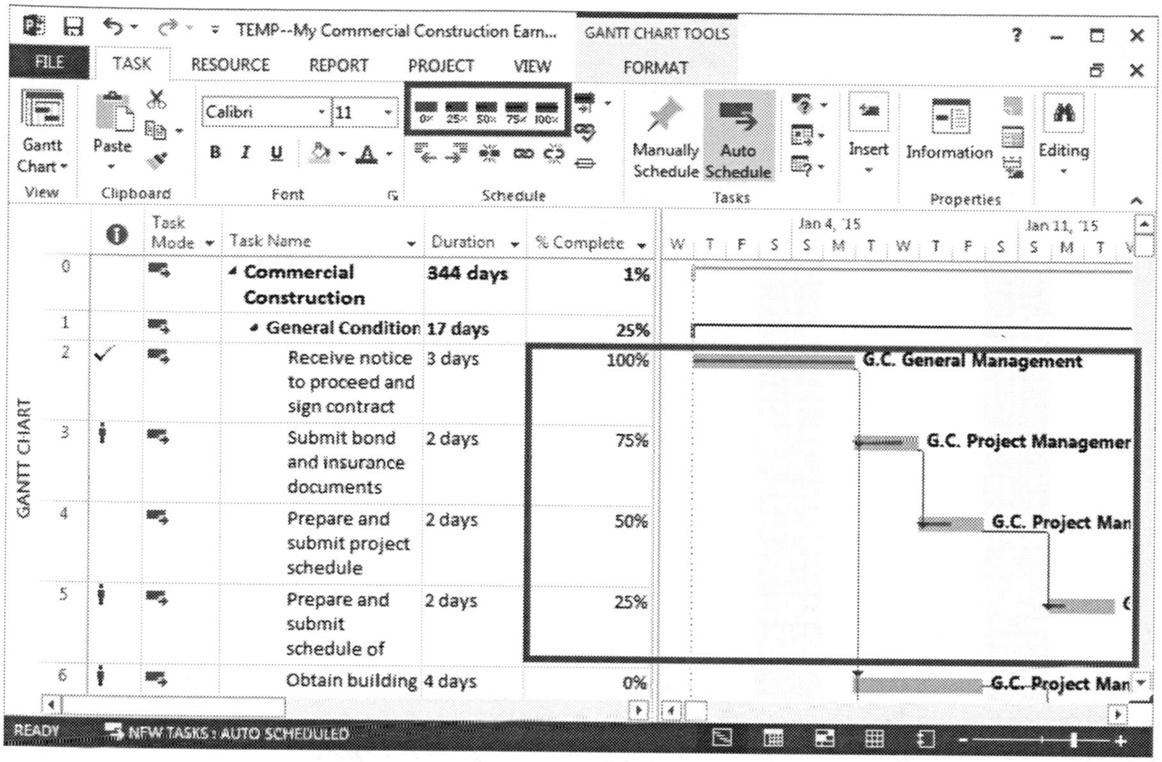

Figure 2-33: Percent complete.

When you set a task's percentage complete, Project 2013 will display a thin progress bar within the task bar on the Gantt Chart. For example, if a task is 50% complete, the Gantt Chart will show a progress bar across half the length of the task bar.

> **Note:** Many project managers determine task percent complete incorrectly. They base the percentage on a subjective estimate of how much work has been accomplished on the task. Instead, you should base the percent complete on an objective measurement of how much of the task's duration has elapsed.

Earned Value Report

You can access the **Earned Value Report** option on the **REPORT** tab of the ribbon, in the **View Reports** command group, in the **Costs** button drop-down menu.

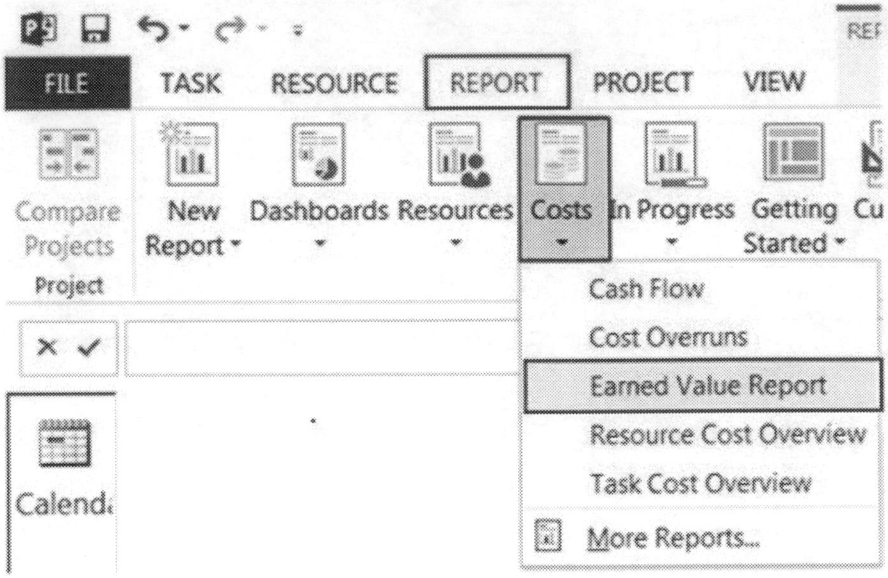

Figure 2-34: Earned Value Report option.

When you select this option, the earned value report will be displayed. You will probably want to customize this report before you share it with the project sponsor or *project stakeholders*.

> **Note:** You'll customize reports later in this course.

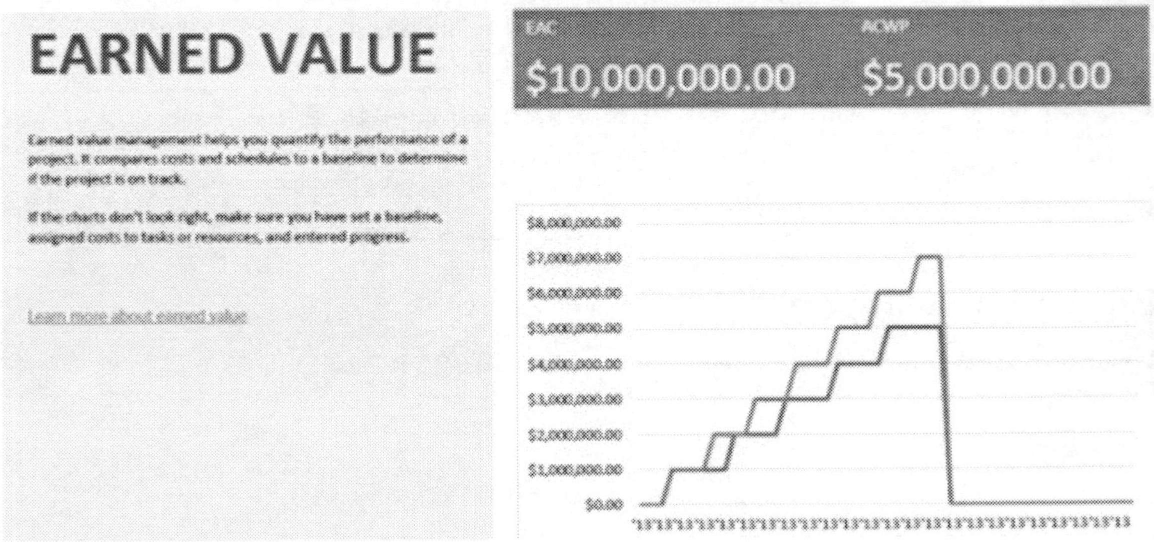

Figure 2-35: Earned value report.

Earned Value Tables

You can access several earned value tables on the **VIEW** tab of the ribbon, in the **Data** command group, in the **Tables** button drop-down menu. When you select this button, you will see several options.

GANTT CHART TOOLS

PROJECT   VIEW   FORMAT   Wind Turbine

- Resource Usage ▾
- Resource Sheet ▾   Sort Outline Tables
- Other Views ▾

Resource Views

▾ Duration ▾ Start

Highlight: [No Highlight]
Filter: [No Filter]
Group by: [No Group]

Built-In

  Cost
✓ Entry
  Hyperlink
  Schedule
  Tracking
  Variance
  Work
  Summary
  Usage

  Reset to Default
  Save Fields as a New Table
  More Tables...

Figure 2-36: Tables button.

More Tables Dialog Box

If you select the **More Tables** option, the **More Tables** dialog box will open. In this dialog box, you can select from three task-related earned value tables and one resource-related earned value table.

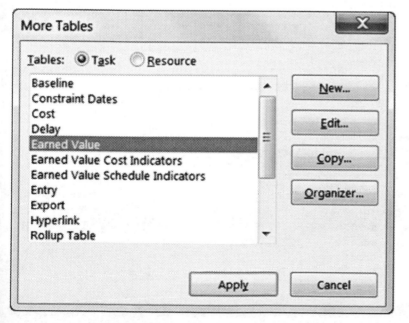

Figure 2-37: More Tables dialog box.

When you select one of these tables it will be displayed in the view pane.

	Task Name	Planned Value - PV (BCWS)	Earned Value - EV (BCWP)	AC (ACWP)	SV	CV	EAC	BAC	VAC
1	Install Turbine 1	$1,000,000.00	$1,000,000.00	$1,000,000.00	$0.00	$0.00	,000,000.00	,000,000.00	$0.00
2	Install Turbine 2	$1,000,000.00	$1,000,000.00	$1,000,000.00	$0.00	$0.00	,000,000.00	,000,000.00	$0.00
3	Install Turbine 3	$1,000,000.00	$1,000,000.00	$1,000,000.00	$0.00	$0.00	,000,000.00	,000,000.00	$0.00
4	Install Turbine 4	$1,000,000.00	$1,000,000.00	$1,000,000.00	$0.00	$0.00	,000,000.00	,000,000.00	$0.00
5	Install Turbine 5	$1,000,000.00	$1,000,000.00	$1,000,000.00	$0.00	$0.00	,000,000.00	,000,000.00	$0.00
6	Install Turbine 6	$1,000,000.00	$0.00	$0.00	000,000.00}	$0.00	,000,000.00	,000,000.00	$0.00
7	Install Turbine 7	$1,000,000.00	$0.00	$0.00	000,000.00}	$0.00	,000,000.00	,000,000.00	$0.00
8	Install Turbine 8	$0.00	$0.00	$0.00	$0.00	$0.00	,000,000.00	,000,000.00	$0.00
9	Install Turbine 9	$0.00	$0.00	$0.00	$0.00	$0.00	,000,000.00	,000,000.00	$0.00
10	Install Turbine 10	$0.00	$0.00	$0.00	$0.00	$0.00	,000,000.00	,000,000.00	$0.00

Figure 2-38: Earned Value table.

> **Note:** You must be in a task-related view (such as **Gantt Chart**) to generate the three task-related earned value tables. Similarly, you must be in a resource-related view (such as **Resource Sheet**) to generate the resource-related earned value table.

> **Note:** To further explore analyzing earned value with Project 2013, you can access the LearnTO **Analyze Earned Value** presentation from the **LearnTO** tile on the LogicalCHOICE Course screen.

Reschedule Uncompleted Work

After you analyze the earned value of your project, you may wish to reschedule uncompleted work to more accurately reflect the actual project finish date. You can do this from the **PROJECT** tab by selecting the **Update Project** command and then selecting the **Rescheduled uncompleted work to start after** option. In most cases you will want the reschedule date to be the same as the status date.

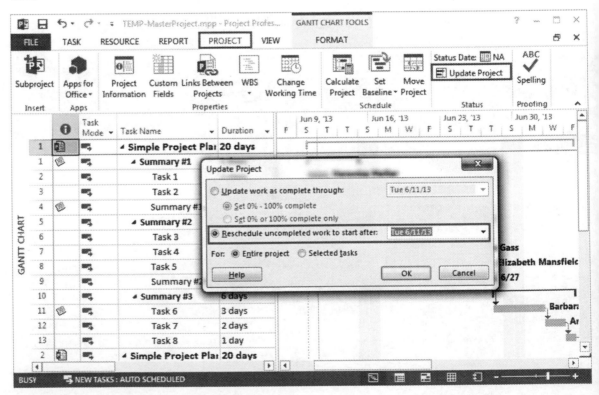

Figure 2-39: Rescheduling uncompleted work.

Note: Taking this action means that your project most likely not finish by the date set in the baseline. Although one of your goals as a project manager is to complete your project on time, uncontrollable factors may make this impossible.

Access the Checklist tile on your LogicalCHOICE course screen for reference information and job aids on How to Determine the Earned Value of a Project

ACTIVITY 2-5
Analyzing Earned Value

Data Files

C:\091111Data\Managing Task Structures\Commercial Construction Earned Value.mpp

Before You Begin

Microsoft Project Professional 2013 is open.

Scenario

The GreeneCentre residential construction project is now three months into execution. Your project sponsor, Sylvia Deaton, has asked for a status report. As you prepare this report, you want to analyze the project's earned value. (During project planning, you entered cost rates for each resource. As soon as the project plan was approved, you baselined the project.)

---

1. Open C:\091111Data\Managing Task Structures\Commercial Construction Earned Value.mpp.

2. Set the project status date for three months from the project start date.
    a) Make sure you are viewing the Gantt Chart.
    b) Select the **PROJECT** tab on the ribbon.
    c) Find the **Status** command group.
    d) Select the **Status Date** button.

    Status Date: 🔲 NA

    e) In the **Status Date** dialog box, in the **Select Date** field, type *4/1/2015*
    f) Select **OK** to close the dialog box.
        On the **PROJECT** tab of the ribbon, the date next to the **Status Date** button reads **4/1/2015**.

    Status Date: 🔲 4/1/15

3. Mark most of the tasks as on track.
    a) In the Gantt Chart, select rows 2–8.
    b) Select the **TASK** tab on the ribbon.
    c) Find the **Schedule** command group.
    d) Select the **Mark on Track** button.

    🔲 Mark on Track ▾

    e) Also mark rows 18–22, 24–30, and 32–35 as on track.
        Notice that check marks appear in the **Indicators** column of the Gantt Chart next to those tasks marked as on track. Also notice that check marks appear next to summary tasks whose subtasks are marked as on track.

---

4. Update the status of other tasks.

   a) Select row 10, **Submit shop drawings and order long lead items - steel.**

   b) Select the drop-down arrow next to the **Mark on Track** button.

      📌 Mark on Track ▾

   c) From the drop-down menu, select the **Update Tasks** option.

      📝 Update Tasks

   d) In the **Update Tasks** dialog box, change the **% Complete** field to *100%* and the **Actual dur** field to *3w*

   e) Select **OK** to close the dialog box.

   f) Also update the status for rows 11–15, changing the **% Complete** fields to *100%* and the **Actual dur** fields to *3w*

      Notice that duration of the tasks has changed from 2 weeks to 3 weeks. Also notice that the **Start** and **Finish** dates of the successor tasks have changed.

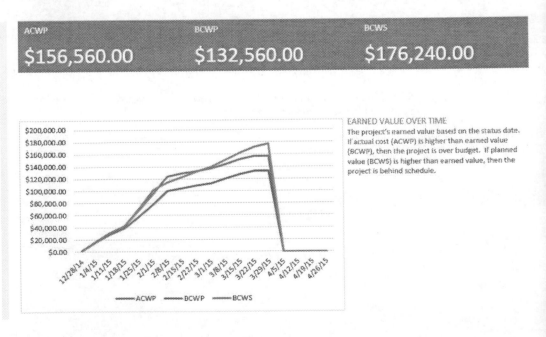

5. Generate an earned value report.

   a) Select the **REPORT** tab on the ribbon.

   b) Find the **View Reports** command group.

   c) Select the **Costs** button.

   d) From the drop-down menu, select **Earned Value Report**.
   Examine the earned value report. Remember that ACWP is the actual cost, BCWP is the earned value, and BCWS is the planned value. Because the actual cost is higher than the earned value, the project is over budget. Because the planned value is higher than the earned value, the project is behind schedule.

ACWP	BCWP	BCWS
$156,560.00	$132,560.00	$176,240.00

EARNED VALUE OVER TIME
The project's earned value based on the status date. If actual cost (ACWP) is higher than earned value (BCWP), then the project is over budget. If planned value (BCWS) is higher than earned value, then the project is behind schedule.

6. Generate an earned value table.

   a) Return to the **Gantt Chart** view.

   b) Select the **VIEW** tab on the ribbon.

   c) Find the **Data** command group.

   d) Select the **Tables** button.

   e) From the drop-down menu, select the **More Tables** option.

   f) In the **More Tables** dialog box, select the **Task** option.

   g) Select **Earned Value.**

   h) Select **Apply** to close the **More Tables** dialog box.
     Examine the **Earned Value** table.

		Task Name	Planned Value - PV (BCWS)	Earned Value - EV (BCWP)	AC (ACWP)	
	0	**Commercial Construction**	$176,240.00	$132,560.00	$156,560.00	
	1	**General Conditions**	$19,360.00	$19,360.00	$19,360.00	
	2	Receive notice to proceed and sign contract	$2,400.00	$2,400.00	$2,400.00	G.C. General Management
	3	Submit bond and insurance documents	$2,000.00	$2,000.00	$2,000.00	G.C. Project Management,G.C. Genera
	4	Prepare and submit project schedule	$2,000.00	$2,000.00	$2,000.00	G.C. Project Management[25%],G.C. !
	5	Prepare and submit schedule of values	$1,760.00	$1,760.00	$1,760.00	G.C. General Management[10%],G.C.
	6	Obtain building permits	$3,200.00	$3,200.00	$3,200.00	G.C. Project Management[50%],G.C. I
	7	Submit preliminary shop drawings	$8,000.00	$8,000.00	$8,000.00	G.C. Project Management[50%],G.(
	8	Submit monthly requests for	$0.00	$0.00	$0.00	

7. Save the file in C:\091111Data\Managing Task Structures as *My Commercial Construction Earned Value.mpp* and then close the file.

Summary

In this lesson, you learned how to manage task structures.

Will you analyze the earned value of your next project? Why or why not?

What do you see as the advantages and disadvantages of network diagramming versus Gantt Charting?

 Note: If your instructor/organization is incorporating social media resources as part of this training, use the LogicalCHOICE Course screen to search for or begin conversations regarding this lesson.

3 | Generating Project Views

Lesson Time: 1 hour

Lesson Objectives

In this lesson, you will generate project views. You will:

- Use the **VIEW** tab on the ribbon.

- Use existing views.

- Create custom views.

- Format and share the Timeline view.

Lesson Introduction

The commands on the **VIEW** tab enable you to control what project information you see and how you see it. So far, you've only worked with a few of the views that are available in Microsoft® Project 2013. There is much more project information you can see with views, and views can be customized to meet your needs. This lesson discusses the many views accessible through the **View Bar,** and several commands on the **VIEW** tab of the ribbon that were not covered in *Microsoft® Project 2013: Part 1.*

TOPIC A

Use View Commands

In this topic, you will use a set of controls that enable you to change how project data is presented in views of your project. All of these controls are found on the **VIEW** tab of the ribbon, in the **Data** command group.

Sort Views

You can use the **Sort** button to arrange the tasks or resources in a different order than they currently appear. When you select this button, a drop-down menu will be displayed. You can choose one of the pre-defined sort criteria (**by Start Date, Finish Date, Cost, Priority,** or **ID**), or you can specify your own sort criteria.

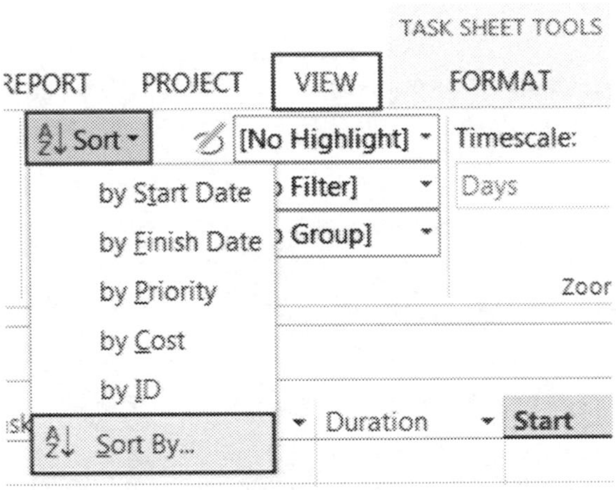

Figure 3-1: Sort button.

If you choose to specify your own sort criteria, the **Sort** dialog box will be displayed. You can use the dialog box to specify up to three fields for sorting data. You can specify whether each field should be sorted in ascending or descending order. You can also specify whether you want tasks permanently renumbered and whether you want to keep the outline structure.

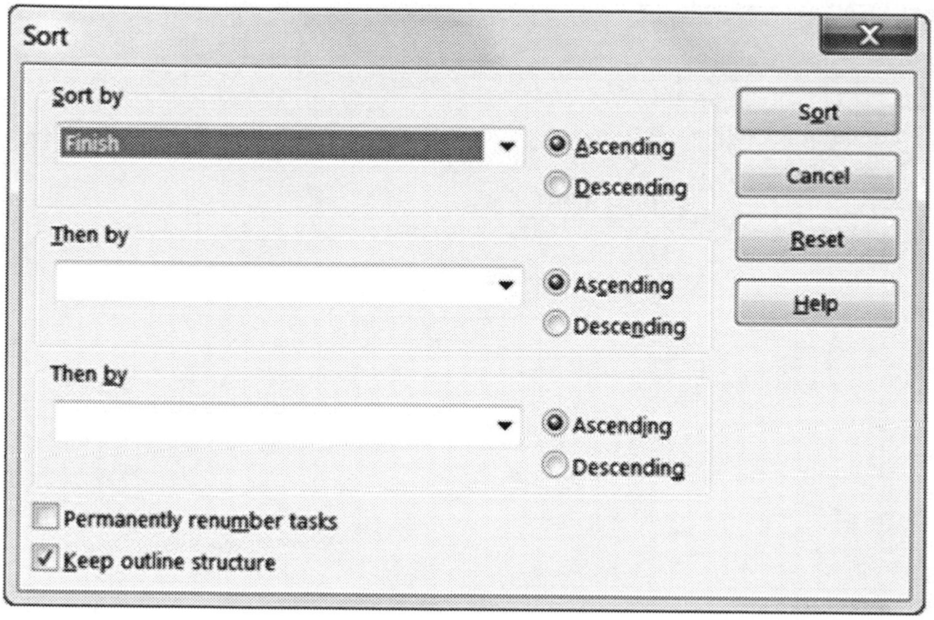

Figure 3-2: Sort dialog box.

Selecting **Sort** sets the sort parameters you changed and closes the dialog box. **Cancel** closes the dialog box without setting the sort parameters you changed. **Reset** returns the sort parameters to their default state.

> **Note:** You can also sort views by selecting the drop-down arrow adjacent to a column header in the view. You can choose to sort the column in ascending or descending order.

Outline Views

You can use the **Outline** button to specify how much detail about the project is shown. This is helpful when your project has summary tasks and subtasks (perhaps several levels for complex projects). When you select this button, a drop-down menu is displayed:

- Selecting the **Show Subtasks** option will display all the subtasks under the currently selected task.
- Selecting the **Hide Subtasks** option will hide all the subtasks under the currently selected task.
- Selecting the **All Subtasks** option will display all of the subtasks in the entire project.
- Selecting the **Level 1** though **Level 9** options will display tasks at the selected level of indentation.

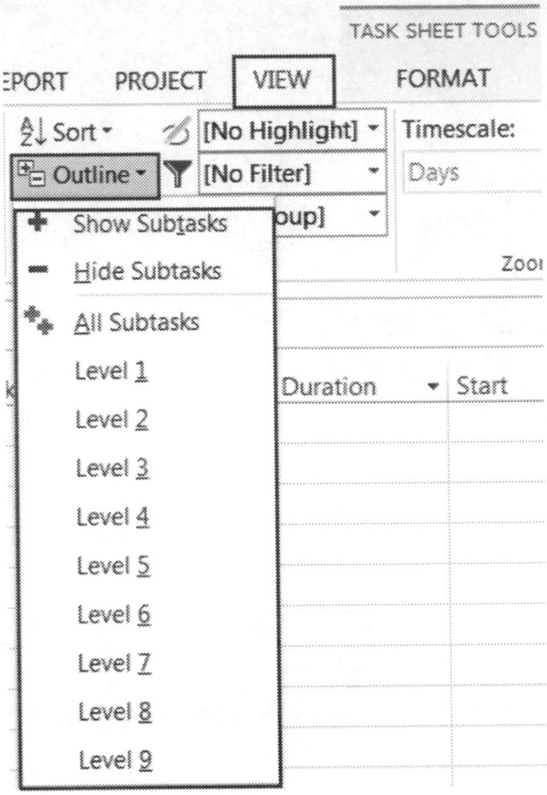

TASK SHEET TOOLS

EPORT   PROJECT   VIEW   FORMAT

Sort ▾   [No Highlight] ▾   Timescale:

Outline ▾   [No Filter] ▾   Days

＋ Show Subtasks

－ Hide Subtasks

✚ All Subtasks

Level 1

Level 2   Duration ▾ Start

Level 3

Level 4

Level 5

Level 6

Level 7

Level 8

Level 9

Figure 3–3: Outline button.

Table Views

You can use the **Tables** button to display different sets of fields in the current view. (Recall that you used the **Tables** button earlier in this course to view variances and generate earned value tables.) When you select this button, a drop-down menu is displayed.

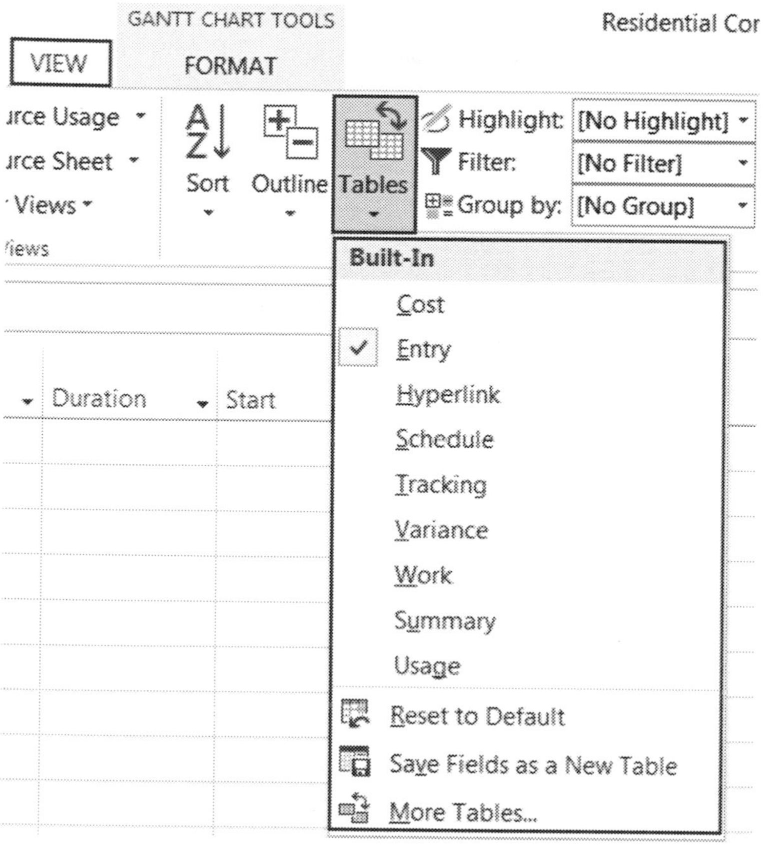

Figure 3-4: Tables button.

The **Entry** table is the default configuration for many views. (This is the configuration you have been using in *Microsoft® Project 2013: Part 1* and *Part 2*). There are several other built-in tables you can choose from this menu, or you can see additional tables by selecting the **More Tables** option. This table explains the use of each of the primary built-in tables.

Table	Use
Cost	To view cost information about project tasks—including baseline, actual, and variance
Hyperlink	To view links to additional task information on a computer, network, or web page.
Schedule	To view schedule information about project tasks—including start dates, finish dates, free slack, and total slack.
Tracking	To view actual task information rather than planned task information.
Variance	To view the difference between baseline and actual dates.
Work	To view the difference between baseline and actual work, as well as work remaining.
Summary	To view basic project information—including task duration, start and finish dates, percent completed, cost, and work.
Usage	To view task work, duration, and start and finish dates.

Tables are not just for viewing project information. You can also use tables to edit existing information or add new information.

You can customize the selected table for your needs (for example, by adding and subtracting columns). You can also use the **Tables** menu to reset a customized table to its default configuration or save it as a new table.

Hyperlink Table

The **Hyperlink** table contains three fields for adding hyperlinks to tasks or resources:

- Use the **Hyperlink** field to enter a name for the hyperlink.
- Use the **Address** field to enter a URL for the hyperlink.
- Use the **SubAddress** field to enter a specific location (such as bookmark) for the hyperlink.

❶	Task Name	Hyperlink	Address	SubAddress
1	Train project managers to use Project 2013	Logical Operations	http://logicaloperations.com/	

Figure 3–5: The Hyperlink table.

Note: Enter a URL into the **Address** field first, and then enter a name into the **Hyperlink** field.

Highlight Views

You can use the **Highlight** field to focus on items in the current view that meet specific criteria. When you select this field, a drop-down list is displayed.

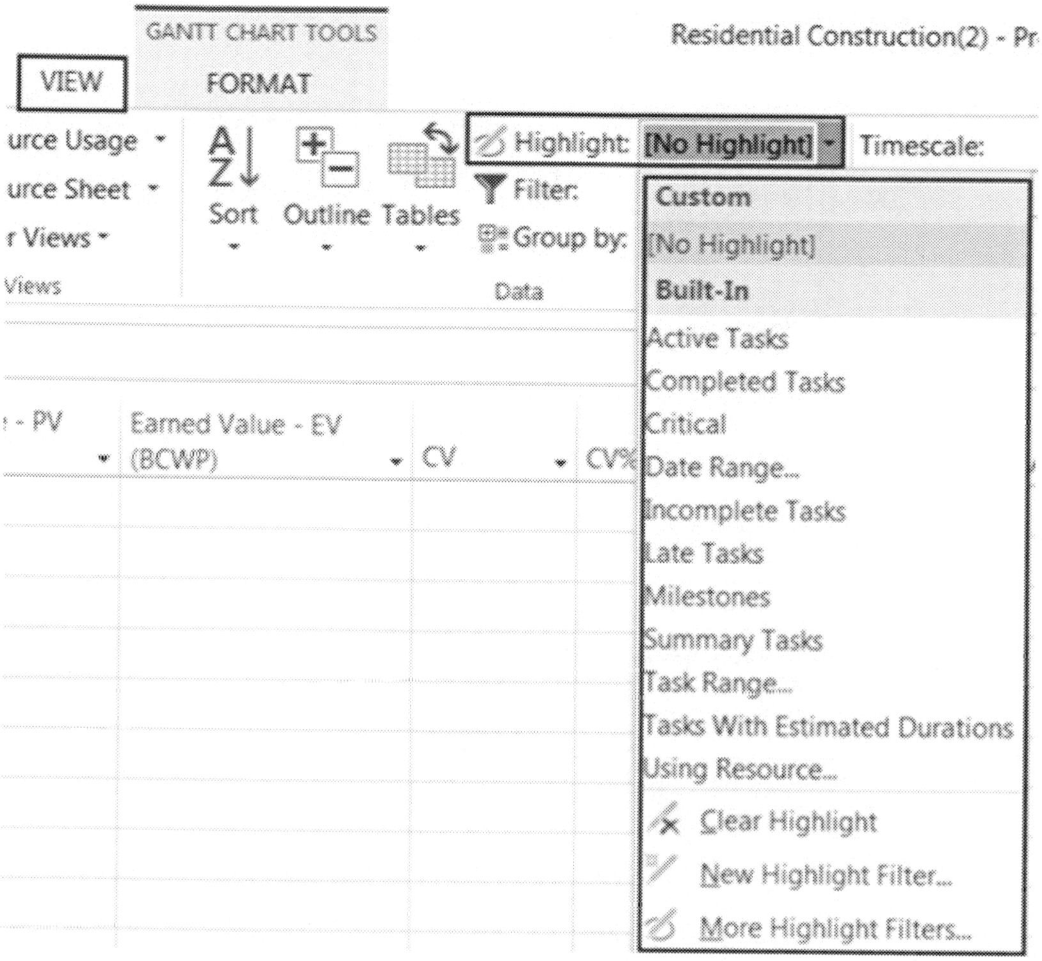

Figure 3–6: Highlight field.

There are several built-in highlight criteria you can choose from this menu, or you can choose other criteria by selecting the **More Highlight Filters** option. Selecting the **Clear Highlight** option will remove highlighting from the current view. If you select the **New Highlight Filter** option, you can create a custom highlight filter.

Filter Views

You can use the **Filter** field to show only items in the current view that meet specific criteria. When you select this field, a drop-down list is displayed.

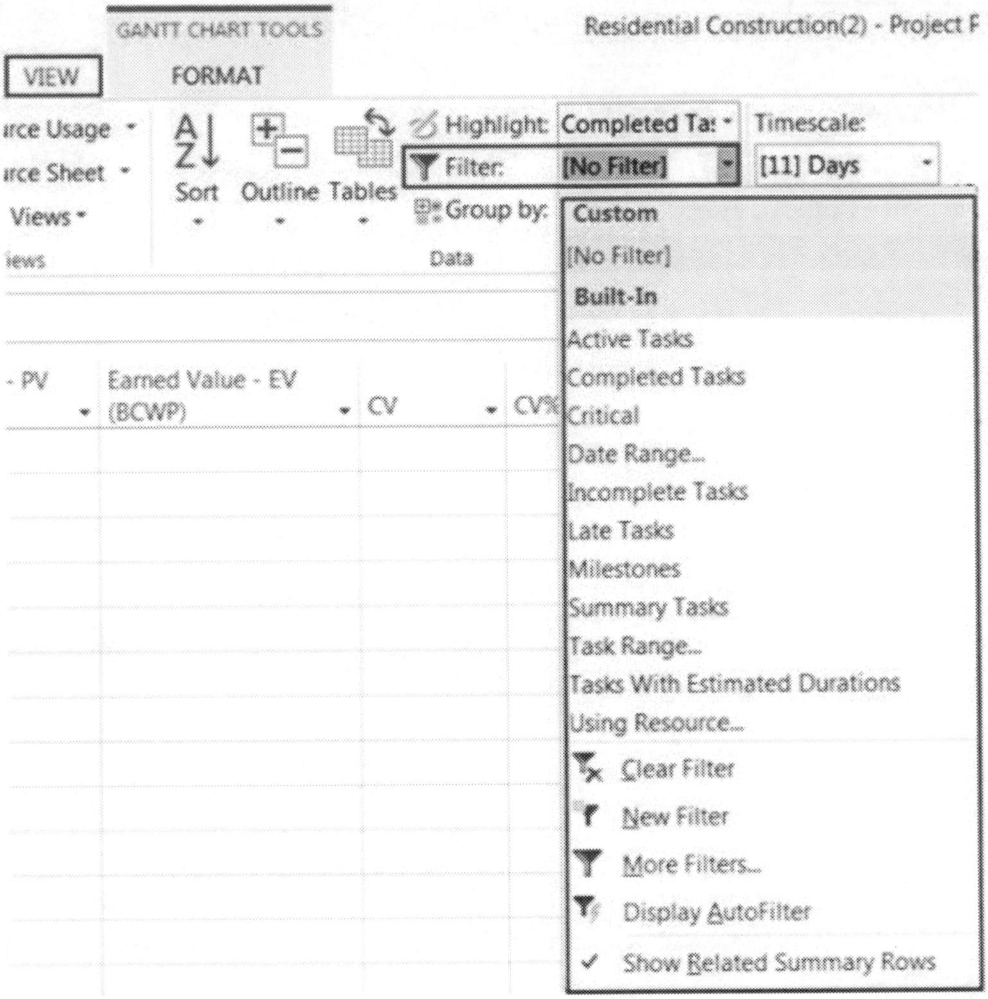

Figure 3-7: Filter field.

There are several built-in filter criteria you can choose from this menu, or you can choose other criteria by selecting the **More Filters** option. Selecting the **Clear Filter** option will remove filtering from the current view. If you select the **New Filter** option, you can create a custom filter. Selecting the **Display AutoFilter** option toggles off and on the ability to apply sorting, filtering, and grouping by selecting the drop-down arrow adjacent to a column header in the view. Selecting the **Show Related Summary Rows** option toggles off and on the display of summary tasks containing subtasks that meet the filtering criteria.

> **Note:** If **Display AutoFilter** is toggled on, you can also filter views by selecting the drop-down arrow adjacent to a column header in the view.

> **Note:** Selecting the **More Highlight Filters** option from the **Highlight** list or the **More Filters** option from the **Filter** list will display the same **More Filters** dialog box. If you close the dialog box with **Highlight,** the view will be highlighted. If you close the dialog box with **Apply,** the view will be filtered.

Group Views

You can use the **Group by** field to group items in the current view that meet specific criteria. When you select this field, a drop-down list is displayed.

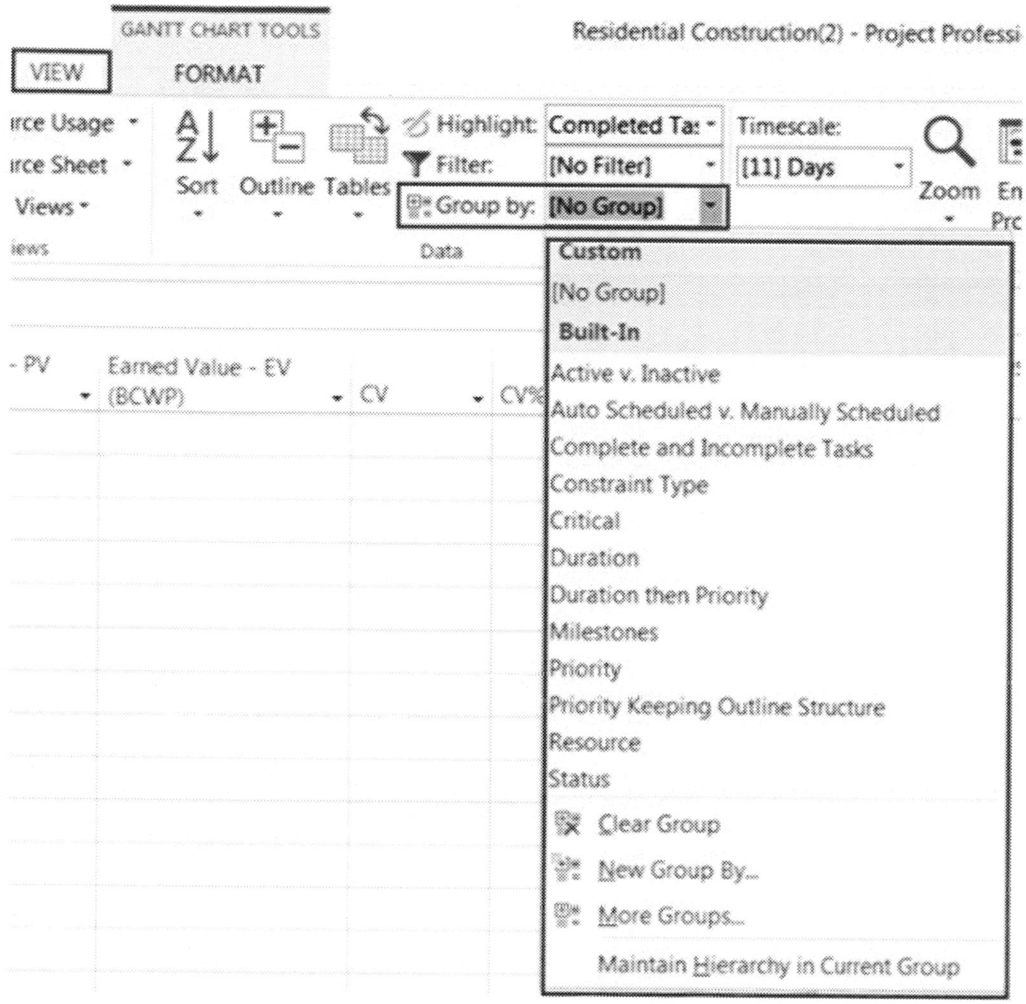

Figure 3–8: Group by field.

There are several built-in grouping criteria you can choose from this menu, or you can choose other criteria by selecting the **More Groups** option. Selecting the **Clear Group** option will remove grouping from the current view. If you select the **New Group By** option, you can create a custom grouping. Selecting the **Maintain Hierarchy in Current Group** option shows summary tasks with their subtasks so that you can see the task hierarchy within the group.

> **Note:** You can also group views by selecting the drop-down arrow adjacent to a column header in the view.

Macros

If you frequently perform the same task in Project 2013, you may want to record a macro to automate the task. The process for recording and using macros in Project 2013 is very similar to that you may have used in other Microsoft® Office® applications. You can find the **Macros** button on **VIEW** tab of the ribbon.

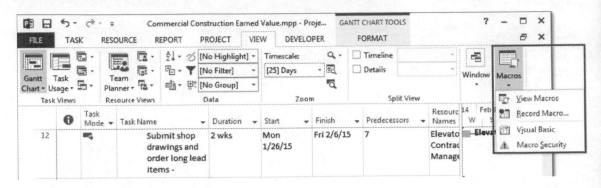

Figure 3-9: Macros command group.

Access the Checklist tile on your LogicalCHOICE course screen for reference
information and job aids on **How to Use View Commands**

ACTIVITY 3-1
Using View Commands

Data Files
C:\091111Data\Generating Project Views\Residential Construction 3.mpp

Before You Begin
Microsoft Project Professional 2013 is open.

Scenario
Your project sponsor, Sylvia Deaton, frequently asks you for details about the GreeneCentre residential construction project. Sylvia realizes it would be more efficient for her to find this information herself in the project plan—which resides on your organization's network. Sylvia has a Project 2013 license on her laptop but is not as familiar with the program as you. You offer to show her how to use some of the commands on the **VIEW** tab to find what she needs.

---

1. Open C:\091111Data\Generating Project Views\Residential Construction 3.mpp.

2. Make sure you are viewing the Gantt Chart.

3. Use the **Sort** command.
   a) Select the VIEW tab on the ribbon.
   b) Find the **Data** command group.
   c) Select the **Sort** button.

   d) From the drop-down menu, select the **Sort By** option.
   e) In the **Sort** dialog box, select the **Sort by** field.
   f) In the **Sort by** drop-down list, select the **Name** option.
   g) Select **Sort** to close the dialog box.
      Notice that the Gantt Chart is now sorted by Task Name.

		Task Mode	Task Name	Duration	Start	Finish	Predece
0			⊿ **Residential Construction**	**152 days**	**Thu 1/1/15**	**Fri 7/31/15**	
35			⊿ **Dry In**	**22 days**	**Mon 5/4/15**	**Tue 6/2/15**	
40			Hang 1st floor exterior doors	1 day	Mon 5/25/15	Mon 5/25/15	39
36			Install 1st floor sheathing	3 days	Tue 5/5/15	Thu 5/7/15	34
41			Install 1st floor windows	3 days	Tue 5/26/15	Thu 5/28/15	40
37			Install 2nd floor sheathing	3 days	Fri 5/8/15	Tue 5/12/15	36
42			Install 2nd floor windows	3 days	Fri 5/29/15	Tue 6/2/15	41
39			Install felt, flashing and shingles	3 days	Wed 5/20/15	Fri 5/22/15	47
38			Install roof decking	3 days	Mon 5/4/15	Wed 5/6/15	33
43			⊿ **Exterior Finishes**	**19 days**	**Wed 6/3/15**	**Mon 6/29/15**	
44			Complete exterior brick	16 days	Wed 6/3/15	Wed 6/24/15	42
45			Complete exterior	3 days	Thu 6/25/15	Mon 6/29/15	44

4. Use the **Outline** command.

a) On the **Quick Access Toolbar,** select the **Undo** button ↶ ˅ to return the Gantt Chart to its original state.

b) On the **VIEW** tab of the ribbon, select the **Outline** button.

Outline
˅

c) From the **Outline** drop-down menu, select the **Level 1** option.
Notice that only the Level 1 summary tasks now show in the Gantt Chart.

	Task Mode	Task Name	Duration	Start	Finish
0		▲ Residential Construction	152 days	Thu 1/1/15	Fri 7/31/15
1	✓	▶ General Conditions	21 days	Thu 1/1/15	Thu 1/29/15
11	✓	▶ Site Work	3 days	Fri 1/30/15	Tue 2/3/15
15	✓	▶ Foundation	42 days	Wed 2/4/15	Thu 4/2/15
24		▶ Framing	22 days	Fri 4/3/15	Mon 5/4/15
35		▶ Dry In	22 days	Mon 5/4/15	Tue 6/2/15
43		▶ Exterior Finishes	19 days	Wed 6/3/15	Mon 6/29/15
46		▶ Utility Rough-Ins and Complete Concrete	21 days	Thu 5/7/15	Thu 6/4/15
55		▶ Interior Finishes	30 days	Wed 6/3/15	Tue 7/14/15
99		▶ Landscaping and Grounds Work	12 days	Mon 7/6/15	Tue 7/21/15
104		▶ Final Acceptance	8 days	Wed 7/22/15	Fri 7/31/15

5. Use the **Tables** command.

   a) On the **Quick Access Toolbar,** select the Undo button to return the Gantt Chart to its original state.

   b) On the **VIEW** tab of the ribbon, select the **Tables** button.

   Tables

   c) From the **Tables** drop-down menu, select the **Usage** option.
   Notice that the **Work** column of the Gantt Chart shows the total amount of time scheduled for all resources assigned to each task.

6. Use the **Highlight** command.

   a) On the **Quick Access Toolbar,** select the **Undo** button to return the Gantt Chart to its original state.

   b) On the **VIEW** tab of the ribbon, select the **Highlight** field. ⬙ Highlight: [No Highlight] ▾

   c) From the **Highlight** drop-down list, select the **Critical** option.
   Notice that the tasks on the critical path are now highlighted in the Gantt Chart.

7. Use the **Filter** command.

   a) On the **Quick Access Toolbar**, select the **Undo** button to return the Gantt Chart to its original state.

   b) On the **VIEW** tab of the ribbon, select the **Filter** field. ▼ Filter: [No Filter] ▼

   c) From the **Filter** drop-down list, select the **Using Resource** option.

   d) In the **Using Resource** dialog box, from the **Show tasks using** drop-down list, select **Architect**.

   e) Select **OK** to close the dialog box.
      Notice that the Gantt Chart now shows only those tasks to which the architect is assigned.

8. Use the **Group by** command.

   a) On the **Quick Access Toolbar,** select the **Undo** button to return the Gantt Chart to its original state.

   b) On the **VIEW** tab of the ribbon, select the **Group by** field. ⊞ Group by: [No Group] ▾

   c) From the **Group by** drop-down list, select the **Milestones** option.
   Notice that the tasks in the Gantt Chart are now grouped by milestones and non-milestones.

9. On the **Quick Access Toolbar**, select the **Undo** button ↶ ˇ to return the Gantt Chart to its original state.

10. Leave *My Residential Construction 3.mpp* open for the next activity.

TOPIC B

Use Existing Views

So far in *Microsoft® Project 2013: Part 1* and *Part 2,* you have learned about a handful of the most commonly used views (such as **Gantt Chart, Resource Sheet, Team Planner,** and **Network Diagram**). In this topic, you'll see all the views that are built into Project 2013. Hopefully you will discover some views that will help you manage your projects more effectively.

Default Views

By default, the **View Bar** displays 13 views that Project 2013 considers to be the most commonly used. Here is a table of those views and what they show. These views are in the order that they appear on the **View Bar.**

View	Description	Use
Calendar	Shows the project schedule in calendar format. You can view tasks by month, week, or by a custom time period.	To see which tasks are scheduled for a particular day or week.
Gantt Chart	Shows project tasks in two ways: as a list, and as bars plotted against the project timeline. You are already very familiar with this view.	To see a list of tasks and a graphical depiction of when they are scheduled to occur.
Network Diagram	Shows the dependencies between tasks. You learned about this view earlier in this course.	To see a graphical depiction of how tasks are sequenced.
Task Form	Shows information about each task, one task per screen.	To work on one task at a time without using the **Task Information** dialog box.
Task Sheet	Shows all of the project tasks as a list. It is similar to the **Gantt Chart** without depicting the tasks as bars plotted against the project timeline.	To see a list of tasks.
Task Usage	Shows how many hours each task or assigned resource is scheduled to use per unit of time shown in the timeline.	To see the number of hours a task or its assigned resources will use in total or for a unit of time.
Timeline	Shows only those tasks you wish to see plotted against the project timeline. This is the same view that is shown by default in the pane above the main view.	To see key tasks in a time plot.
Tracking Gantt	Shows baseline and scheduled Gantt bars for each task.	To compare the baseline schedule with the actual schedule.
Resource Form	Shows information about each resource, one resource per screen.	To work on one resource at a time without using the **Resource Information** dialog box.
Resource Graph	Shows what percentage of each resource is being used per unit of time shown in the	To see when each resource is allocated and overallocated.

View	Description	Use
	timeline, one resource per screen. Overallocated resources appear in red.	
Resource Sheet	Shows all of the project resources as a list. You are already familiar with this view.	To see a list of all project resources and detailed information about each one.
Resource Usage	Shows as a table all of the resources, which tasks each resource is assigned, and how many hours each task is scheduled to take per unit of time shown in the timeline.	To see a list of all resources and the tasks to which each resource is assigned.
Team Planner	Shows in a graph all the resources and the tasks to which each resource is assigned per unit of time shown in the timeline. Overallocated resources appear in red. You should already be familiar with this view.	To see a graphical depiction of each resource, the tasks to which each is assigned, and when each resource will work on its assigned tasks.

More Views

In addition to the 13 views shown on the **View Bar,** there are 14 others from which you can choose. Here is a table of those views and what they show.

View	Description
Bar Rollup	Shows only summary tasks.
Descriptive Network Diagram	Shows more information for each node than in the regular network diagram.
Detail Gantt	Shows more information about each task bar than in the regular Gantt Chart, including the critical path.
Gantt with Timeline	Shows the **Timeline** view in the upper pane and the **Gantt Chart** view in the lower pane.
Leveling Gantt	Shows schedule delays caused by resource leveling.
Milestone Date Rollup	Shows all tasks concisely labeled with milestone marks and dates on summary Gantt bars.
Milestone Rollup	Shows all tasks concisely labeled with milestone marks on summary Gantt bars.
Multiple Baselines Gantt	Shows a Gantt Chart with baselines for all tasks displayed against the timeline.
Relationship Diagram	Shows each task, one task per screen, along with its predecessors and successors and the type of dependencies it has with its predecessors and successors.
Resource Allocation	This is a split view that shows the **Resource Usage** view in the top pane. When a task is selected, a Gantt Chart of just that task is shown in the bottom pane.
Resource Name Form	This view is similar to the **Resource Form** view, but shows less detail about the resource.
Task Detail Form	This view is similar to the **Task Form** view, but shows more detail about the task.

View	Description
Task Entry	This is a split view that shows the **Gantt Chart** view in the top pane and the **Task Form** view in the bottom pane. When you select a task in the upper pane, its information is shown in the bottom pane.
Task Name Form	This view is similar to the **Task Form** view, but shows less detail about the task.

More Views Option and Dialog Box

To see these views, select the **More Views** option at the bottom of the **View Bar.** The **More Views** dialog box will open. Choose the view you wish to display and select **Apply.**

 Note: The **New, Edit, Copy,** and **Organizer** buttons in the **More Views** dialog box will be discussed in the next topic.

 Access the Checklist tile on your LogicalCHOICE course screen for reference information and job aids on How to Use Existing Views

ACTIVITY 3-2
Using Existing Views

Before You Begin
My Residential Construction 3.mpp is open.

Scenario
It is now four months into implementation of the GreeneCentre residential construction project. You would like to check the status of the project by viewing it in several different ways.

1. Use the **Calendar** view.

   a) On the **View Bar,** find and select the **Calendar** button.

   b) In the **Calendar** view, below the **Month** button, select the right arrow several times to advance the month to **May 2015.**
   Notice which tasks are scheduled for May 2015.

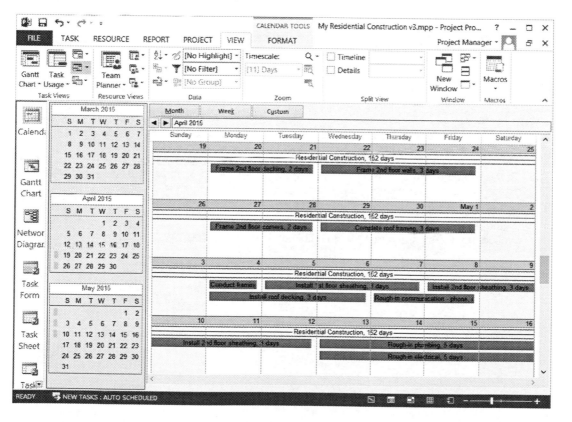

2. Use the **Task Form** view.

   a) On the **View Bar,** find and select the **Task Form** button.

   b) In the **Task Form** view, in the upper-right corner, select **Next** twice to advance the task **Name** to **Finalize plans and develop estimate with owner, architect.**
   Notice that the task is 100% complete, and that four resources were assigned to the task.

3. Use the **Resource Form** view.

   a) On the **View Bar,** find and select the **Resource Form** button.

   > **Note:** You may need to select the down arrow at the bottom of the **View Bar** to find the button.

   b) In the **Resource Form** view, in the upper-right corner, select **Next** several times to advance the resource **Name** to **Architect.**

   c) In the **Std rate** field, change $0.00/h to *$100.00/h*

   d) In the upper-right corner, Select **OK.**
   Notice that the standard rate for the architect now reads $100.00/h.

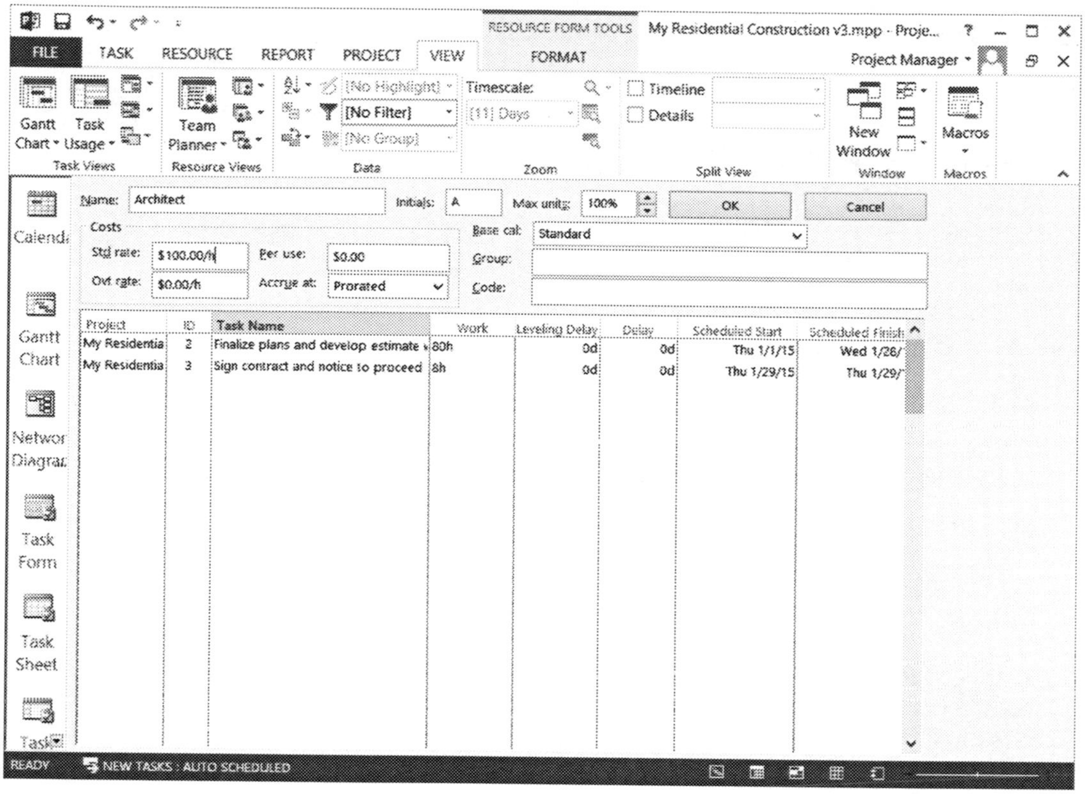

4. Save and close the Project file.

TOPIC C

Create Custom Views

Even though Project 2013 provides you with 27 built-in views, you may need to build your own to show the information you want about your project. In this topic, you will create custom views.

New Views

You can begin to create a new view by selecting **New** in the **More Views** dialog box.

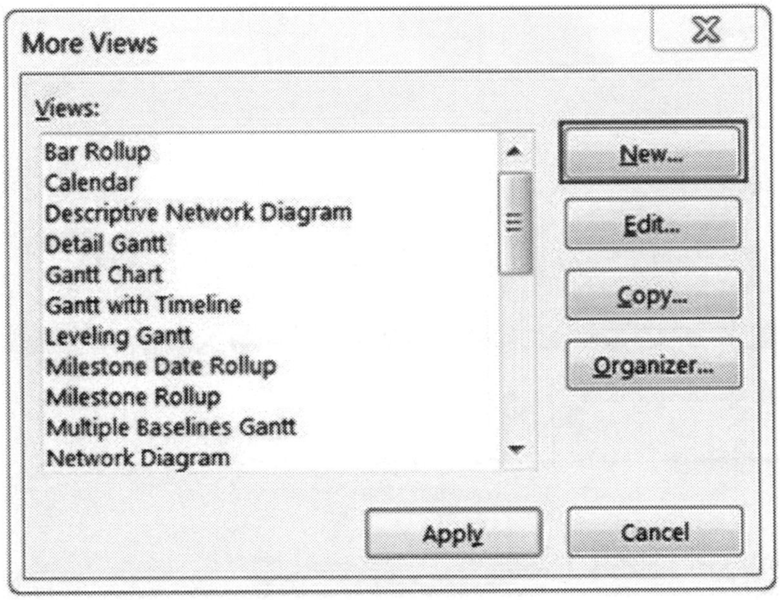

Figure 3-10: New button in the More Views dialog box.

Define New View Dialog Box

The **Define New View** dialog box will be displayed. You have the option creating a **Single view** or a **Combination view**.

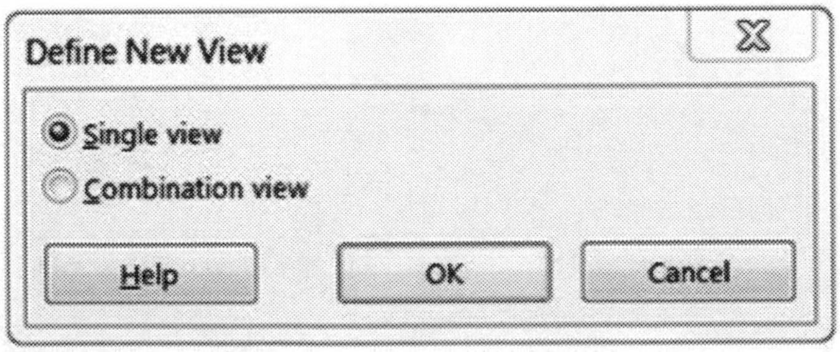

Figure 3-11: Define New View dialog box.

Select **Single view** if you only want to see project information in a single pane. Select **Combination view** if you want to see overall project information in one pane and details about selected items in another pane.

Single View

If you select **Single view,** a **View Definition** dialog box will be displayed.

![View Definition in 'Project1' dialog box showing fields: Name (View 1), Screen (Gantt Chart), Table, Group, Filter, with checkboxes Highlight filter and Show in menu checked, and buttons Help, OK, Cancel.]

Figure 3-12: View Definition dialog box for a new single view.

Use the **View Definition** dialog box to configure the view:

- Specify a **Name** for the new view.
- Select a **Screen** (a previously existing view) upon which the new view will be based.
- Select a **Table** that will be applied to the new view.
- Select a **Group** that will be applied to the new view.
- Select a **Filter** that will be applied to the new view.
- Choose whether to add highlighting for the filter in the new view.
- Choose whether to show the new view in the menu.

 Note: The **Screen** you choose as the basis for your new view may constrain your choices in the **Table, Group,** and **Filter** fields. You may need to make a selection in each field to close the dialog box, or you may not be able to make selections in some fields.

Combination View

If you select **Combination view,** a different **View Definition** dialog box will be displayed.

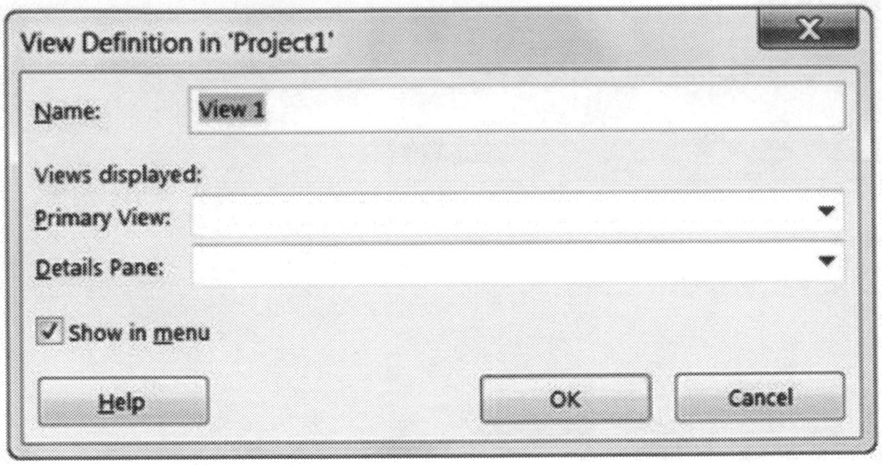

Figure 3-13: View Definition dialog box for a new combination view.

In this **View Definition** dialog box, you have different options to configure the view:

- Specify a **Name** for the new view.
- Select a **Primary View** to include in the main pane of the new view.
- Select a second view to include in the **Details Pane** of the new view.
- Choose whether to show the new view in the menu.

Edit Views

In many cases, you may find that editing a built-in view is more efficient than creating a new view. You can edit a built-in view (or a new view) by selecting **Edit** in the **More Views** dialog box.

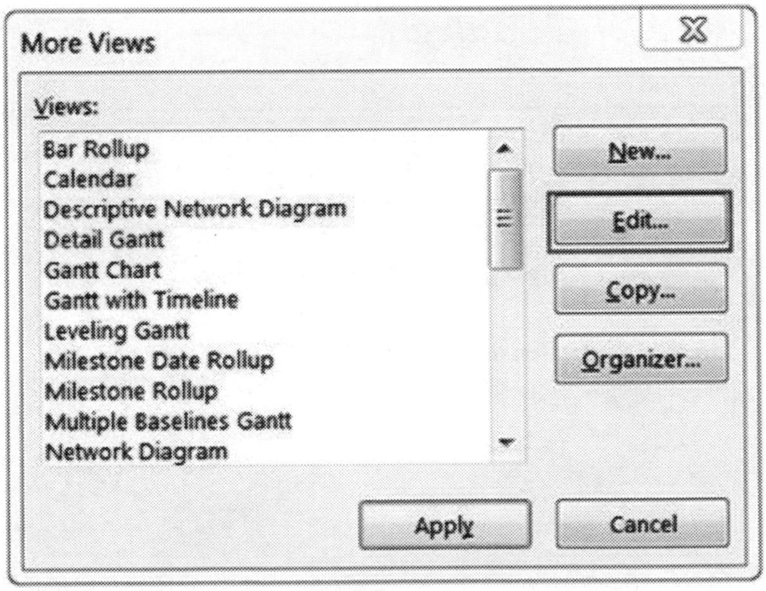

Figure 3-14: Edit button in the More Views dialog box.

Selecting **Edit** will open a **View Definition** dialog box similar to one for new views.

Copy Views

If you want to edit a built-in view, it's a good idea to make a copy of it first so that the original view is unchanged. You can copy a built-in view (or a new view) by selecting **Copy** in the **More Views** dialog box.

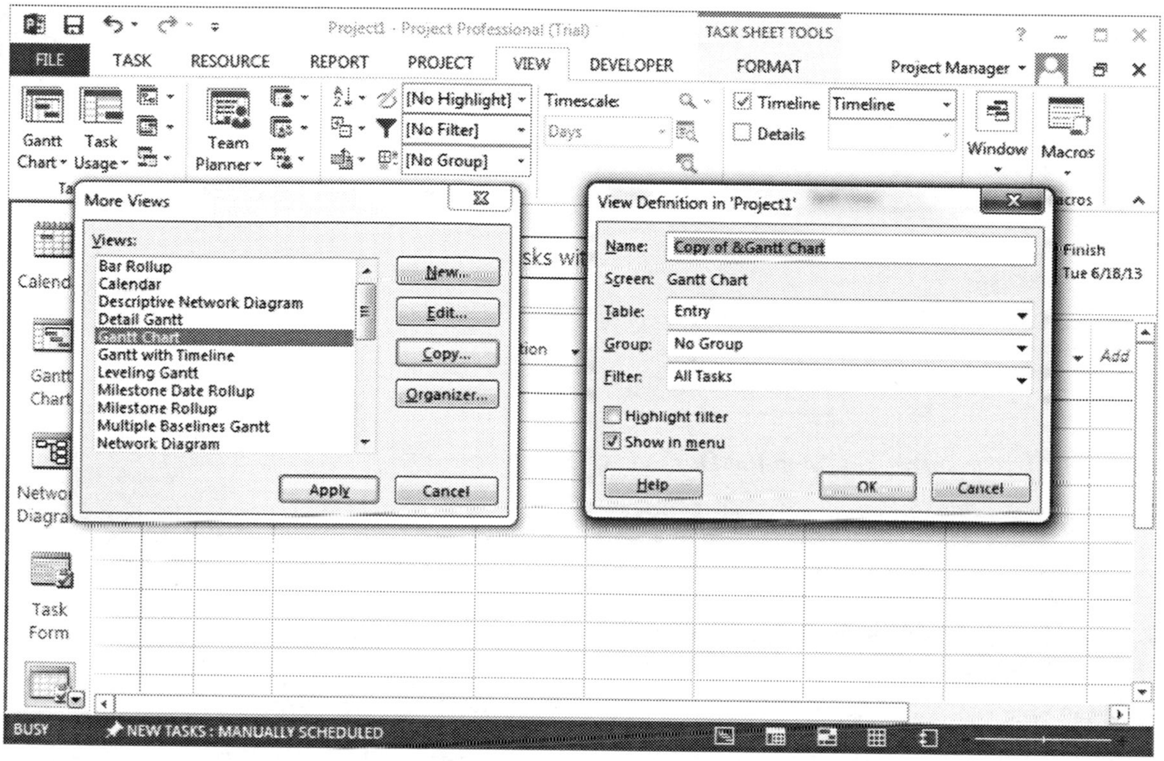

Figure 3-15: Copy button in the More Views dialog box.

Selecting **Copy** will open a **View Definition** dialog box similar to one for new views.

> **Note:** To further explore customizing Project 2013 views, you can access the LearnTO **Customize Views** presentation from the **LearnTO** tile on the LogicalCHOICE Course screen.

The Organizer

You can organize built-in or new views by selecting **Organizer** in the **More Views** dialog box.

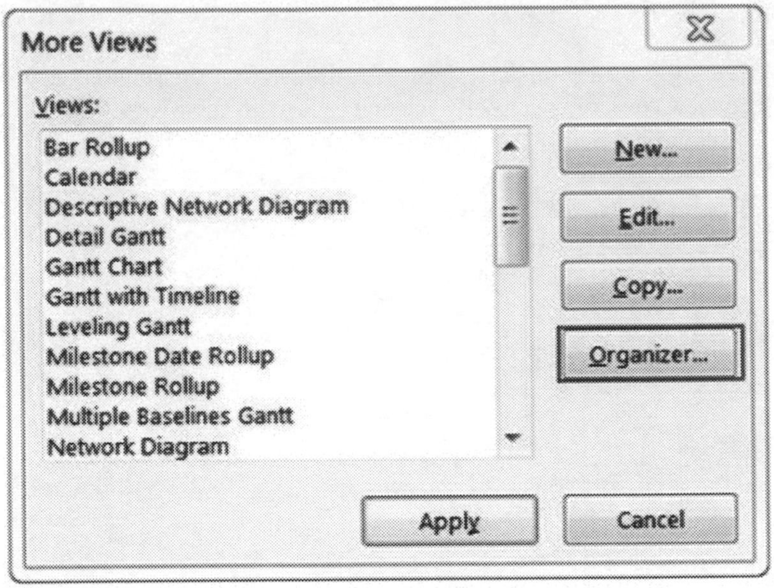

Figure 3-16: Organizer button in the More Views dialog box.

This will open the **Organizer** dialog box to the **Views** tab.

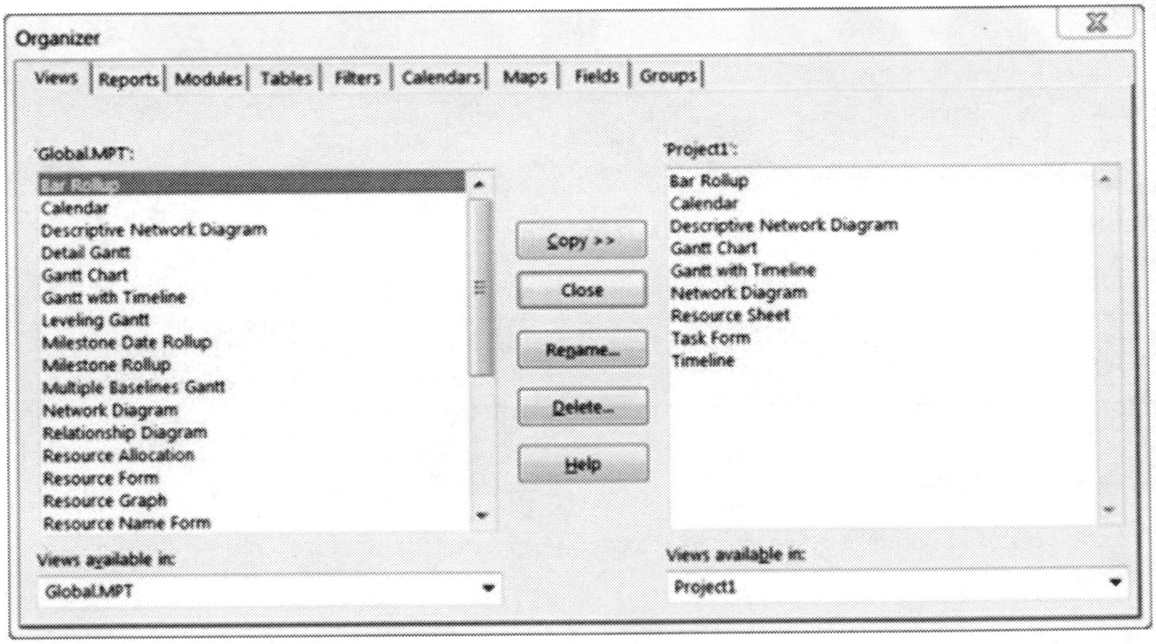

Figure 3-17: Organizer dialog box.

On the left side of the **Views** tab, you will see a list of all the views that are available in the main Microsoft Project Template file (**Global.MPT**). On the right side of the **Views** tab, you will see a list of all the views that are available in the Project 2013 file that is open. Between the lists is a set of command buttons:

- **Copy** enables you to copy the selected view from one list to the other.
- **Cancel** or **Close** closes the **Organizer** dialog box.
- **Rename** enables you to give the selected view another name.
- **Delete** removes the selected view.

Note: Take care when deleting views from **Global.MPT.** Generally speaking, you do not want to delete any of Project 2013's built-in views.

Format Views

Sometimes, a selected view does not display the project information you want to see, the way you want it to see it. Project 2013 allows you to change what a view shows, and how the view shows it, using view format controls. These controls can be especially useful when you intend to share a view as a printed document or as a PDF/XPS file.

Whenever you are in a view, its formatting controls will be displayed in a **FORMAT** contextual tab. Every view has its own set of formatting controls. For example, the formatting tools for the **Gantt Chart** view are much different than those for the **Network Diagram** view.

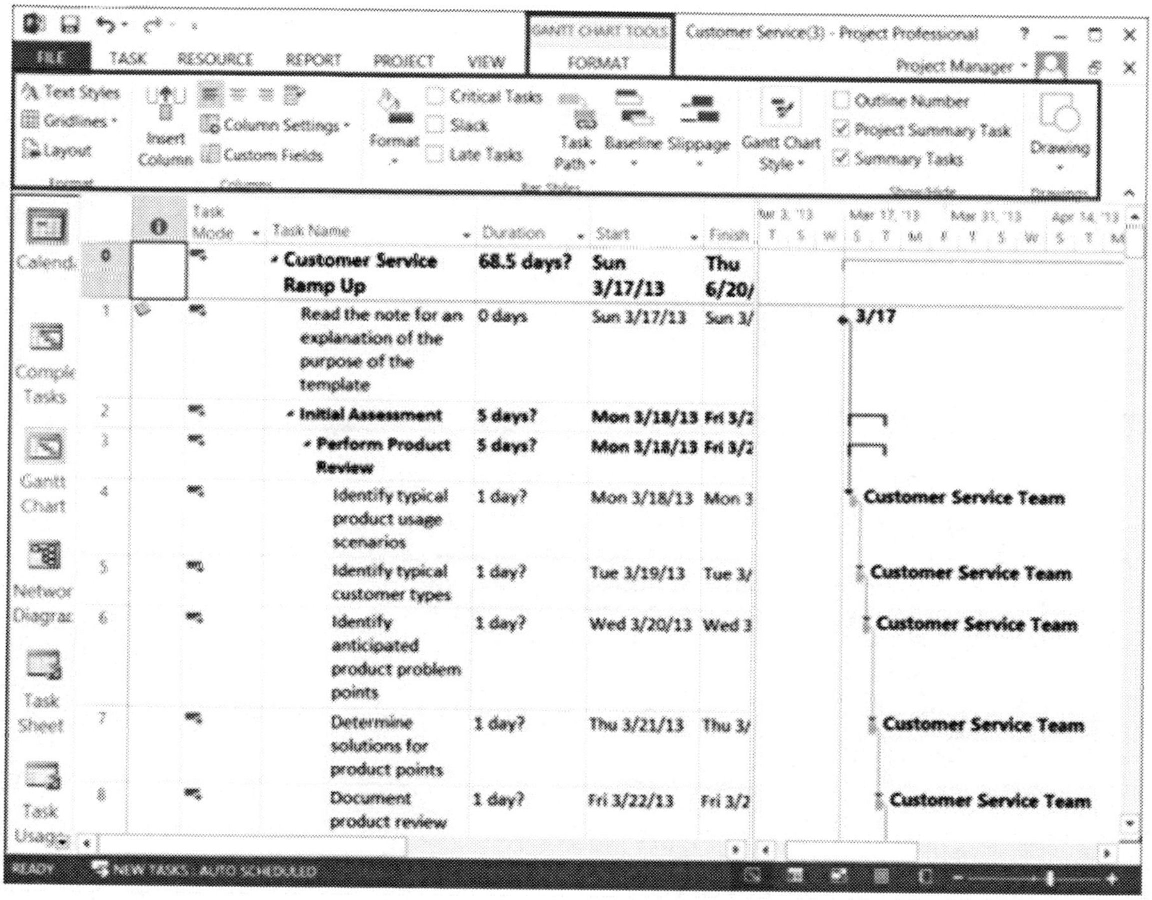

Figure 3-18: GANTT CHART TOOLS FORMAT contextual tab.

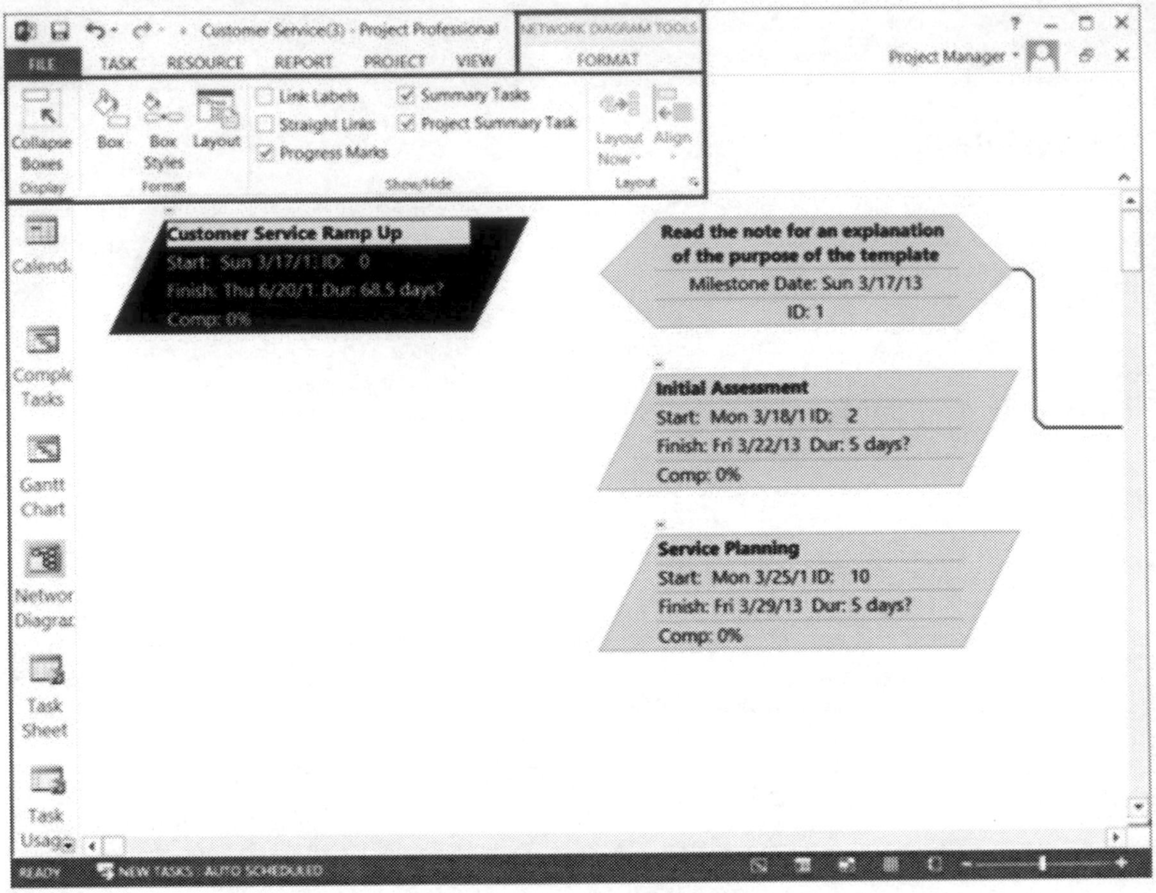

Figure 3-19: NETWORK DIAGRAM TOOLS FORMAT contextual tab.

Note: Due to the variability and number of view formatting controls, this course will not cover them in more depth except for the **Timeline** view, which will be discussed later in this course. You may want to experiment with the other view formatting controls.

Access the Checklist tile on your LogicalCHOICE course screen for reference information and job aids on How to Create a Custom View

ACTIVITY 3–3
Creating Custom Views

Data Files

C:\091111Data\Generating Project Views\Commercial Construction 3.mpp

Before You Begin

Microsoft Project Professional 2013 is open.

Scenario

It is now six months into implementation of the GreeneCentre commercial construction project. Overall, the project is on schedule and within budget. About a third of the tasks have been completed. You would like to see a list of pending tasks without the completed tasks. You would also like to see a list of completed tasks without the pending tasks, and the details for a single selected task. You decide to create a new single view and a new combination view.

---

1. Open C:\091111Data\Generating Project Views\Commercial Construction 3.mpp.

2. Create a new single view.
   a) Scroll down to the bottom of the **View Bar**.
   b) Select the **More Views** button.
   c) In the **More Views** dialog box, select **New**.
   d) In the **Define New View** dialog box, select **Single view** and select **OK**.
   e) In the **View Definition** dialog box, in the **Name** field, type *My Incomplete Tasks*
   f) In the **Screen** field, select **Gantt Chart** from the drop-down list.
   g) In the **Table** field, select **Entry** from the drop-down list.
   h) In the **Group** field, select **No Group** from the drop-down list.
   i) In the **Filter** field, select **Incomplete Tasks** from the drop-down list.
   j) Leave the **Highlight filter** box unchecked.
   k) Leave the **Show in menu** box checked.

l) Select **OK** to close the **View Definition** dialog box.

m) Select **Apply** to close the **More Views** dialog box.
    Notice that your new view is displayed, showing only uncompleted tasks.

3. Create a new combination view.

a) Scroll down to the bottom of the **View Bar**.

b) Select the **More Views** button.

c) In the **More Views** dialog box, select **New**.

d) In the **Define New View** dialog box, select **Combination** view and select **OK**.

e) In the **View Definition** dialog box, in the **Name** field, type *My Completed Tasks*

f) In the **Primary View** field, select **Completed Tasks** from the drop-down list.

g) In the **Details Pane** field, select **Task Form** from the drop-down list.

h) Leave the **Show in menu** box checked.

i) Select **OK** to close the **View Definition** dialog box.

j) Select **Apply** to close the **More Views** dialog box.
Notice that your new view is displayed, showing only completed tasks. Also notice that, when you select a task in the top pane, its details appear in the bottom pane.

4. Save the file in C:\091111Data\Generating Project Views as *My Commercial Construction 3.mpp* and then close the file.

TOPIC D

Format and Share the Timeline View

Microsoft® Project 2013 includes a very useful tool—the **Timeline** view—that allows you see your project's "big picture" and easily share it with your stakeholders. The **Timeline** view allows you to take a snapshot of key tasks and milestone, which you can then paste into other Microsoft® Office programs.

Timeline View

In *Microsoft® Project 2013: Part 1,* you were briefly introduced to the **Timeline** view as a component of the Project 2013 interface. By default, whenever you create a new Project file, the **Timeline** view will be visible as a secondary, horizontal pane below the ribbon. You can make the **Timeline** smaller or larger by sliding the divider bar at the bottom of the **Timeline** pane up or down. You can even completely hide the **Timeline** by sliding the divider bar all the way up.

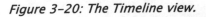

Figure 3–20: The Timeline view.

> **Note:** If the **Timeline** is hidden, you can unhide it by selecting the **VIEW** tab, finding the **Split View** command group, and checking the **Timeline** field.

You also learned in *Microsoft® Project 2013: Part 1,* that you can control which tasks are displayed on the **Timeline** by checking and unchecking the **Display on Timeline** field in the **Task Information** dialog box. Generally speaking, you should show high-level summary tasks on the **Timeline.** However, there may be circumstances when you want to show important, lower-level tasks.

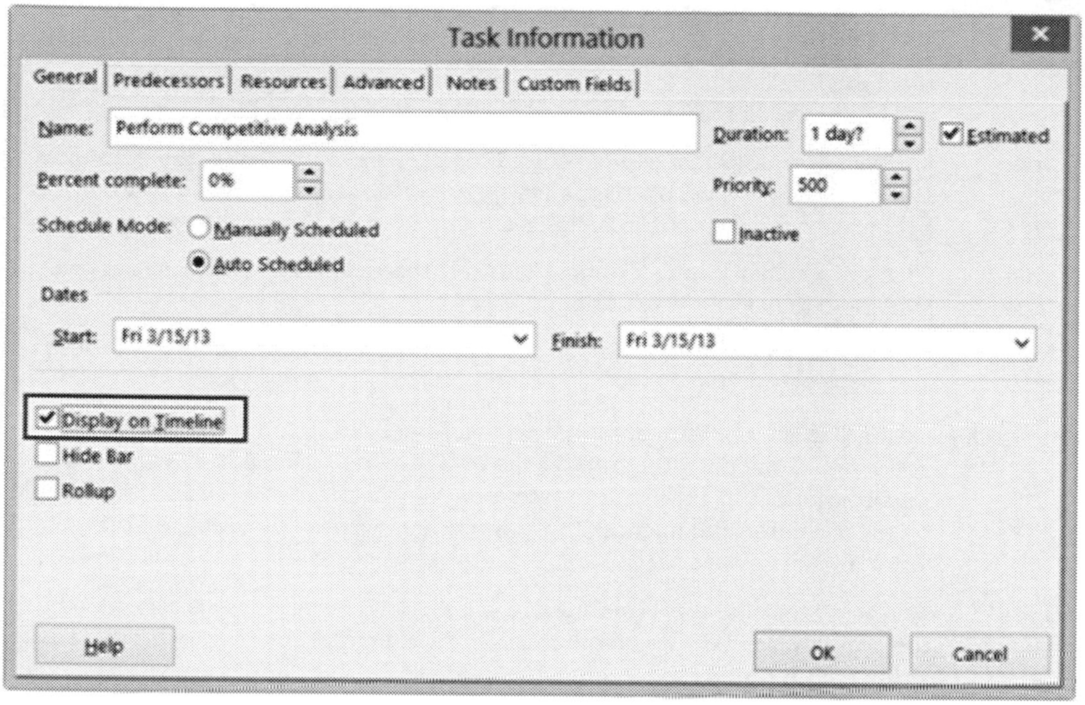

Figure 3-21: Display on Timeline field in Task Information dialog box.

Earlier in this course, you learned that you can access the **Timeline** view using **View Bar**. If you select this option, the **Timeline** will be displayed as the primary pane of the interface.

Format the Timeline

Whenever you select a pane containing the **Timeline** view, Project 2013 will display the **TIMELINE TOOLS FORMAT** contextual tab on the ribbon. These controls enable you to change how the **Timeline** displays.

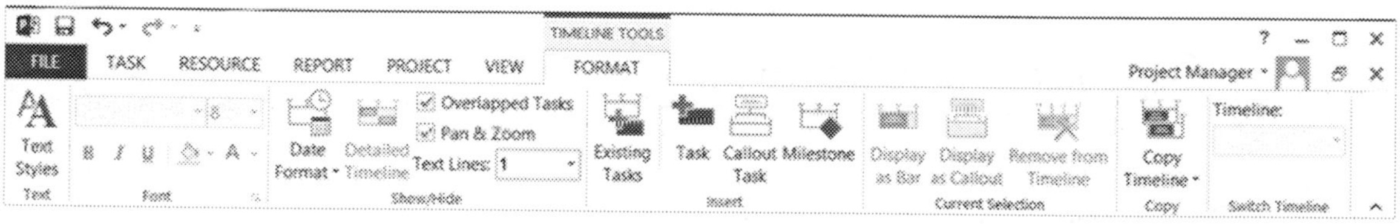

Figure 3-22: TIMELINE TOOLS FORMAT contextual tab.

Here is a table of the commands on this tab and what they do.

Command	Description
Text Styles	Changes the font, size, color, and other attributes of all text on the **Timeline**.
Font Command Group	Changes the font, size, color, and other attributes of selected text on the **Timeline**.
Date Format	Changes how dates arc displayed and which dates are displayed on the **Timeline**.
Detailed Timeline	Changes how much detail is displayed on the timeline. This command is only active when the **Timeline** is visible as a secondary pane below the ribbon. If the command is toggled off, most of the text will be hidden on the **Timeline** and

Command	Description
	the **Timeline** height will be shorter. If the command is toggled on, more text will be shown on the **Timeline** and the **Timeline** height will be taller.
Overlapped Tasks	Changes how tasks that overlap chronologically are displayed on the **Timeline**. If this field is checked, overlapping tasks are displayed on different rows. If this field is unchecked, overlapping tasks are displayed on the same row.
Pan & Zoom	Changes whether **Pan & Zoom** is active. If this field is checked, you can pan and zoom to navigate the **Timeline** view.
Text Lines	Changes the height of task bars in the **Timeline**. The minimum is 1 (shortest) and maximum is 10 (tallest).
Existing Tasks	Changes which tasks are displayed on the **Timeline**. If you select this button, Project 2013 will open the **Add Tasks to Timeline** dialog box, which shows all the project tasks in a dynamic outline You can check tasks you want to be visible on the **Timeline** and uncheck those you do not want to be visible on the **Timeline**.
Insert Task	Adds a new task to the **Timeline** as a bar chart. (This new task is also added to the project's task list.) If you select this button, Project 2013 will open the **Task Information** dialog box.
Insert Callout Task	Adds a new task to the **Timeline** as a callout. (This new task is also added to the project's task list.) This command is only active when the **Timeline** is visible as the primary pane. If you select this button, Project 2013 will open the **Task Information** dialog box.
Insert Milestone	Adds a new milestone task to the **Timeline**. (This new milestone is also added to the project's task list.) This command is only active when the **Timeline** is visible as the primary pane. If you select this button, Project 2013 will open the **Task Information** dialog box.
Display as Bar	Changes whether a selected task on the **Timeline** is displayed as a bar. You must select a task before this command is active. If the selected task is not displayed as a bar, it will be displayed as a callout.
Display as Callout	Changes whether a selected task on the **Timeline** is displayed as a callout. You must select a task before this command is active. If the selected task is not displayed as a callout, it will be displayed as a bar.
Remove from Timeline	Removes the selected task from the **Timeline**. You must select a task before this command is active. Removing a task from the **Timeline** does not delete the task from the project.
Copy Timeline	Provides various option for you to copy the **Timeline**.

> **Note:** The **Copy Timeline** option will be discussed in the next section.

Share the Timeline

Whenever you select the **Copy Timeline** button on the **TIMELINE TOOLS FORMAT** contextual tab, Project 2013 gives you three options for copying the timeline.

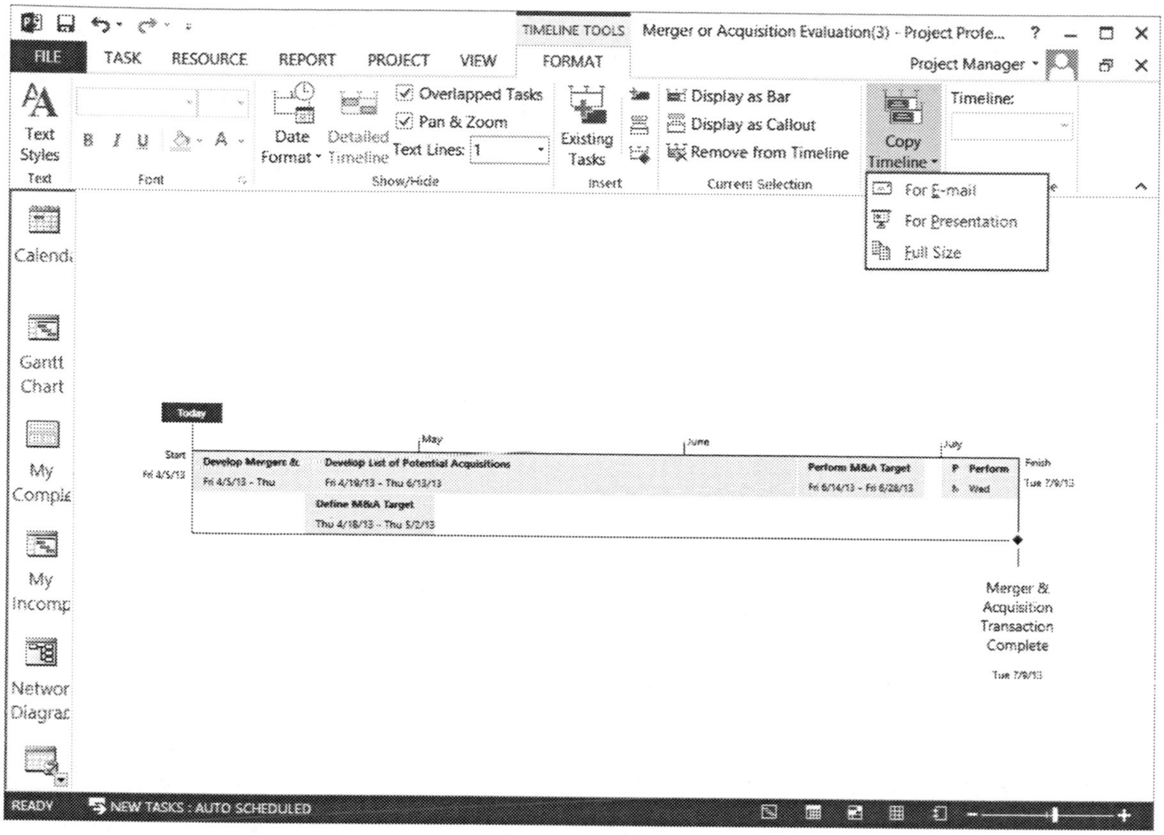

Figure 3-23: Copy Timeline options.

Here is a table of the options and how to use them.

Option	Use
For E-mail	Copies the **Timeline** to the Windows clipboard so that you can paste it into the body of an Outlook® email message. The pasted image will be relatively small in both visual and data size. The pasted image may not look exactly like the copied **Timeline**.
For Presentation	Copies the **Timeline** to the Windows clipboard so that you can paste it into a PowerPoint® slide. The pasted image will be larger in both visual and data size. Again, the pasted image may not look exactly like the copied **Timeline**.
Full Size	Copies the **Timeline** to the Windows clipboard at its current zoom level—be it large, medium, or small. You can paste it into any Office document. You may find this option especially useful for Word, Publisher®, or Visio® documents you plan to print. The visual and data size of the pasted image depends on the zoom level of the copied **Timeline**. The pasted image will look exactly like the copied **Timeline**.

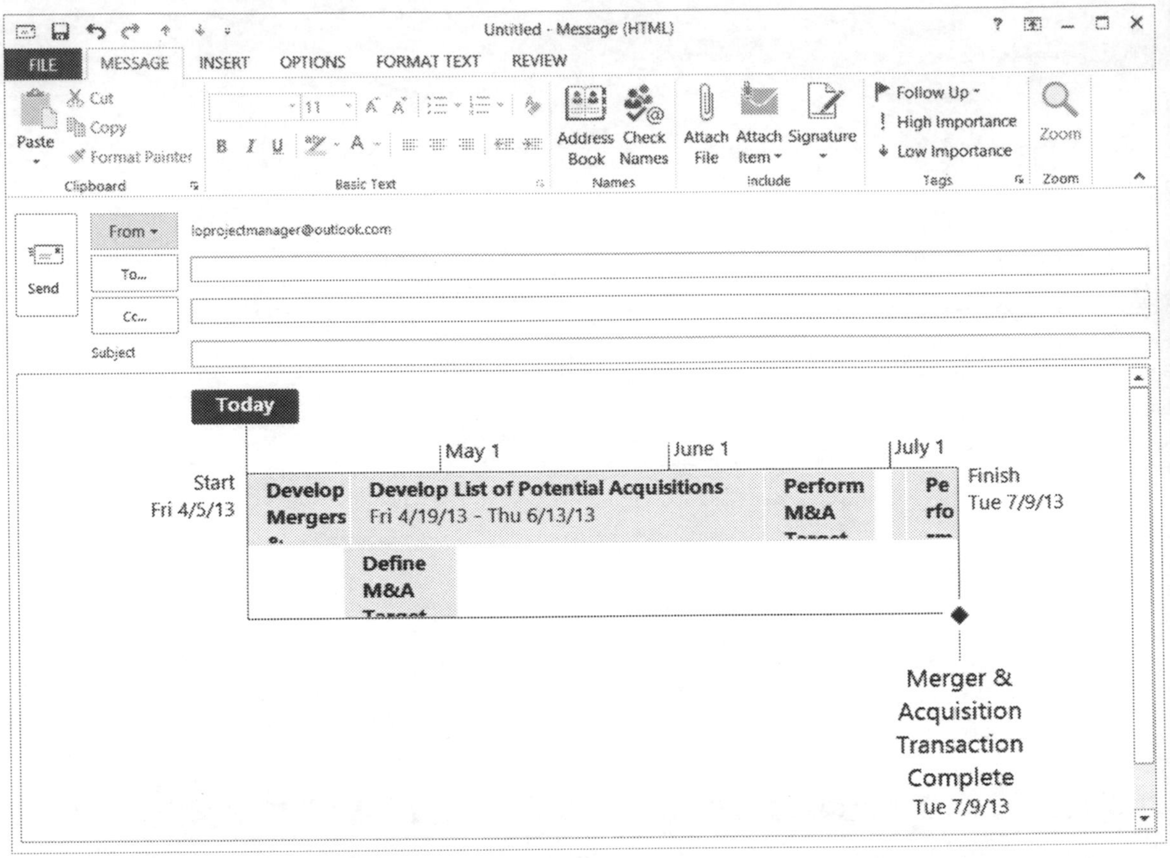

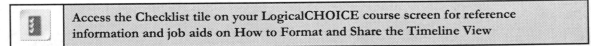

Figure 3–24: Timeline pasted into Outlook email message.

Access the Checklist tile on your LogicalCHOICE course screen for reference information and job aids on How to Format and Share the Timeline View

ACTIVITY 3-4
Formatting and Sharing the Timeline

Data Files

C:\091111Data\Generating Project Views\Commercial Construction 3.mpp

Before You Begin

Microsoft Project Professional 2013 is open.

Scenario

The monthly GreeneCentre commercial construction project team meeting will take place next Monday. During the meeting, you plan to give an oral and written report of the project. For the oral report, you want to put the project timeline into a PowerPoint slide. For the written report, you want to put the project timeline into a Word document.

---

1. Open **C:\091111Data\Generating Project Views\Commercial Construction 3.mpp**.

2. Format the **Timeline**.

   a) Select the **Timeline** view in the upper pane.

   You may want to slide the pane divider down so that the **Timeline** view pane is about the same size as the Gantt Chart view pane.

b) In the **TIMELINE TOOLS FORMAT** contextual tab, select the **Text Styles** button. In the **Text Styles** dialog box, change the font for the entire **Timeline** from Segoe UI to Lucida Console. Change the font size for the entire **Timeline** from 8 to 9. Select OK to close the dialog box.
Notice that the font has changed in the entire **Timeline**.

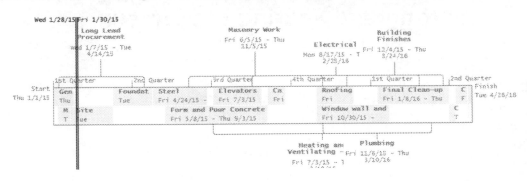

c) Select the **Date Format** button. In the drop-down, change the **Format** from **Default** to **1/28**. Notice that the month and day (but not the year) are displayed on the **Timeline**.

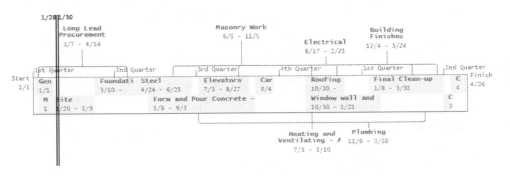

d) Select the **Text Lines** field. Change the number from **1** to **2**. Notice that the task rows are taller.

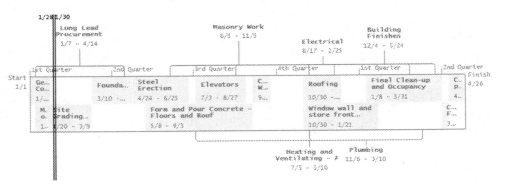

e) Select the **Long Lead Procurement** callout. Select the **Display as Bar** button. Notice that the task has become a bar.

f) Select the **Steel Erection** bar. Select the **Display as Callout** button. Notice that the task has become a callout.

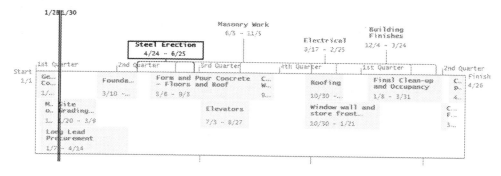

3. Copy the **Timeline** from Project and paste it into PowerPoint®.

   a) Select the **Copy Timeline** button. From the drop-down select the **For Presentation** option.
   b) From the Windows 8 **Start** screen, open Microsoft PowerPoint 2013.
   c) In the PowerPoint **Welcome Center**, select the **Blank Presentation** option.
   d) On the first slide, select **Click to add title** and type *GreeneCentre Commercial Construction*
   e) Also on the first slide, select **Click to add subtitle** and add *Monthly Project Team Meeting*

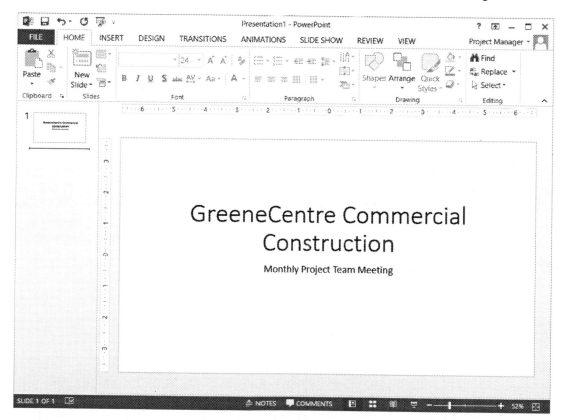

   f) Select the **New Slide** button on the **HOME** tab of the ribbon.
   g) On the new slide, select **Click to add title** and type *Timeline*
   h) Also on the new slide, select the **Click to add text** content box. On the ribbon, on the **HOME** tab, select the arrow under the **Paste** button, and from the drop-down, select the **Picture** option. Notice that an image of the **Timeline** has been added to the slide.

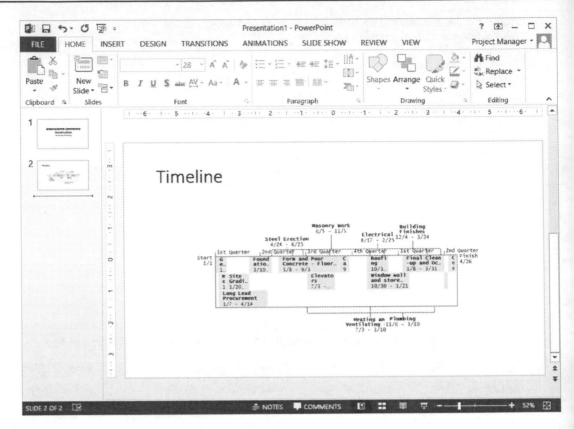

4. Copy the **Timeline** from Project and paste it into Word.
   a) Switch back to Project.
   b) On the ribbon, on the **FILE** tab, select the **Copy Timeline** button. From the drop-down, select the **Full Size** option.
   c) From the Windows 8 **Start** screen, open Microsoft Word 2013.
   d) In the Word **Welcome Center,** select the **Blank document** option.
   e) Select the **PAGE LAYOUT** tab on the ribbon. Select the **Margins** button and choose the **Narrow** option. Select the **Orientation** button and choose the **Landscape** option.
   f) Select the **HOME** tab. At the top of the document, type *GreeneCentre Commercial Construction* and select the **Title** style from the ribbon.
   g) On a new line below the title, type *Monthly Project Team Meeting* and select the **Subtitle** style from the ribbon.
   h) On a new line below the title, type *Timeline* and select the **Heading 1** style from the **HOME** tab of the ribbon.

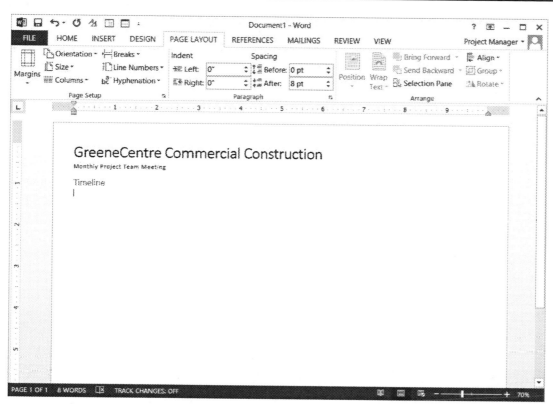

i) Add a new line below **Timeline**. Select the **Paste** button on the **HOME** tab of the ribbon.
    Notice that an image of the **Timeline** has been added to the document. You may want to change the
    zoom level on the **Status Bar** to see the entire timeline.

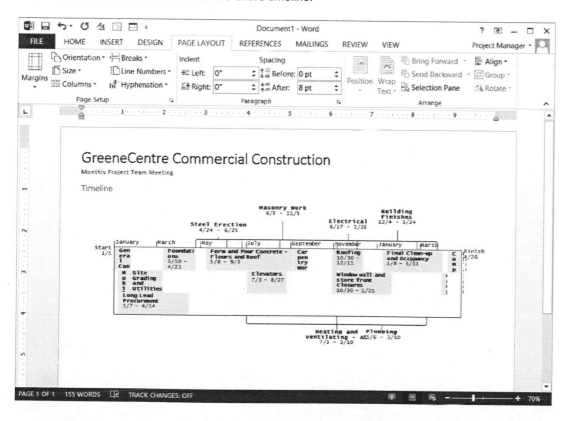

5. Save the Project file in C:\091111Data\Generating Project Views as *My Timeline.mpp* and then close it.
    Save the PowerPoint file in C:\091111Data\Generating Project Views as *My Timeline.pptx* and then

close it. Save the Word file in C:\091111Data\Generating Project Views as *My Timeline.docx* and then close it.

Summary

In this lesson, you learned how to generate project views.

Which of Project 2013's built-in views do you find most useful, and why?

Which custom view are you most likely to build, and why?

 Note: If your instructor/organization is incorporating social media resources as part of this training, use the LogicalCHOICE Course screen to search for or begin conversations regarding this lesson.

4 Producing Project Reports

Lesson Time: 1 hour

Lesson Objectives

In this lesson, you will produce project reports. You will:

- Create project reports from existing templates.

- Generate and customize a new report.

- Export a report with the **Visual Reports** tool.

Lesson Introduction

Microsoft® Project 2013 reports empower you to monitor your project during execution so that you can take corrective action if needed. The commands on the **REPORT** tab enable you to generate new reports and customize existing reports to meet your needs.

Earlier in this course, you encountered the earned value report. In this lesson, you will use other reports in Project 2013. The reporting capabilities of Project 2013 are vastly improved over earlier versions, enabling you to see and share the status of a project clearly and compellingly.

TOPIC A

Use Existing Reports

Project 2013 has 20 built-in reports, all of which you can access from the **REPORT** tab on the ribbon. These built-in reports are grouped into four types: **Dashboards, Resources, Costs,** and **In Progress.** In this topic, you will explore each group.

Dashboard Reports

Dashboards are eye-catching, dynamic reports that show important project indicators.

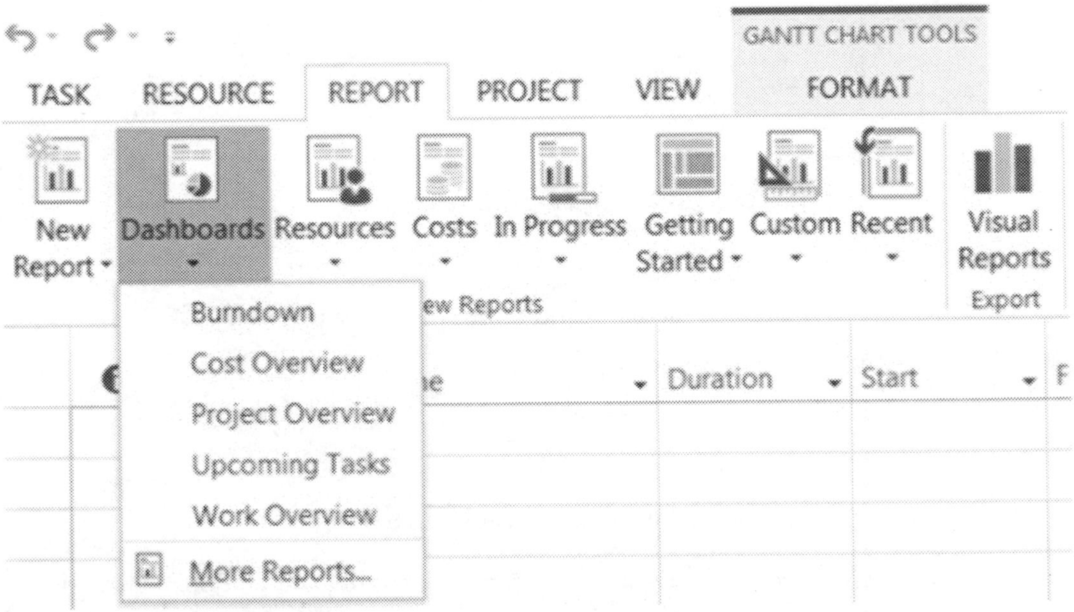

Figure 4–1: View Dashboard Reports button.

Types of Dashboard Reports

There are five dashboard reports.

Report	Description	Use
Burndown	Shows two side-by-side line charts. The **Work Burndown** chart depicts how much work you have completed and how much you have left. If the remaining cumulative work line is steeper, then the project may be late. The **Task Burndown** chart depicts how many tasks you have completed and how many you have left. If the remaining tasks line is steeper, then your project may be late.	To see if your project is ahead of schedule, on time, or late.
Cost Overview	Shows three charts and tables depicting the status of project costs. The **Progress Versus Cost** shows progress made versus the cost spent over time. If the **% Complete** line is below the cumulative cost line, your project may be over budget. The **Cost Status** table shows the cost status for top-level tasks. The **Cost Status** chart also shows the cost status for top-level tasks graphically.	To see if your project is under budget, on budget, or over budget.

Report	Description	Use
Project Overview	Shows three charts and tables depicting the status of project tasks. The **% Complete** chart shows the status for all top-level tasks. The **Milestone Due** table shows milestones that are coming soon. The **Late Tasks** table shows tasks that are past due.	To see how much of your project is complete.
Upcoming Tasks	Shows two charts and tables depicting tasks with start or finish dates within the next week. The **Tasks Starting Soon** table shows the status of tasks starting in the next 7 days. The **Remaining Tasks** chart shows the status of tasks that are due in the next 7 days.	To see how much of your project remains to be done.
Work Overview	Shows four charts depicting work and resource data. The **Work Burndown** chart was described previously. The **Work Stats** chart shows work stats for all top-level tasks. The **Resource Stats** chart shows work stats for all your resources. The **Remaining Availability** chart shows the remaining availability for all work resources.	To see how much work has been completed and how much work remains to be done.

Resource Reports

Resource reports show important resource information about your project.

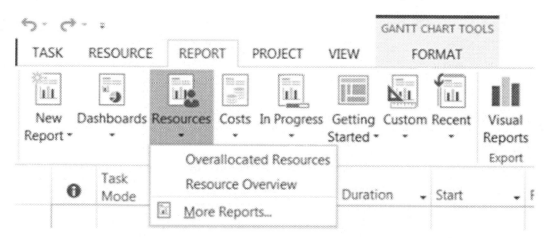

Figure 4–2: View Resource Reports button.

Types of Resource Reports

There are two resource reports.

Report	Description	Use
Overallocated Resources	Shows two charts depicting information about overallocated resources. The **Work Status** chart shows the actual and remaining work for overallocated resources. The **Overallocation** chart shows surplus work assigned to overallocated resources.	To see which resources are assigned more work than they can accomplish.
Resource Overview	Shows three charts and tables depicting information about project resources. The **Resource Stats** chart shows the work status for all work resources. The **Work Status** chart shows the percent of work done by all the	To see the status of all your project resources.

Report	Description	Use
	work resources. The **Resource Status** table shows the remaining work for all work resources.	

Cost Reports

Cost reports show important cost information about your project..

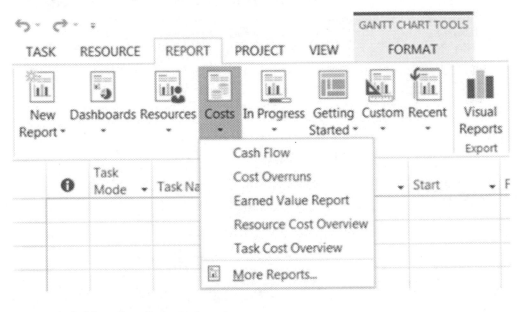

Figure 4–3: View Cost Reports button.

Types of Cost Reports

There are five cost reports.

Report	Description	Use
Cash Flow	Shows two charts and tables depicting project costs. The chart shows the project's cumulative cost and the cost per quarter. The table shows cost information for all top-level tasks.	To see how much money you've spent on the project.
Cost Overruns	Shows four charts and tables depicting project overspending on tasks and resources. The **Task Cost Variance** chart and table show cost variance for all top-level tasks in the project. The **Resource Cost Variance** chart and table show cost variance for all work resources in the project.	To see which tasks and resources are over budget.
Earned Value Report	As discussed earlier in the course, shows a chart depicting earned value compared to the budgeted cost of work scheduled (BCWS) and the actual cost of work performed (ACWP).	To see if the project is behind schedule or over budget.
Resource Cost Overview	Shows two charts and a table depicting resource costs. The **Cost Status** chart shows the cost status for work resources. The **Cost Distribution** chart shows how costs are spread out amongst different resource types. The **Cost Details** table shows cost information for all work resources in the project.	To see the cost status of project resources.

Report	Description	Use
Task Cost Overview	This is similar to the **Resource Cost Overview** report, but shows task information rather than resource information.	To see the cost status of project tasks.

In Progress Reports

Progress reports show how your active tasks and pending milestones are performing.

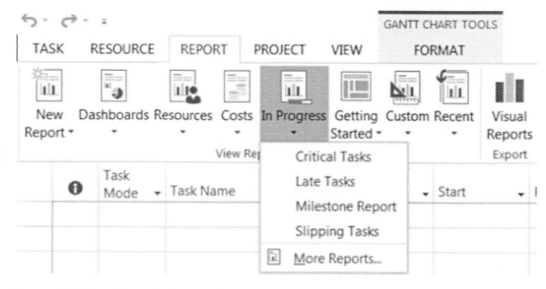

Figure 4-4: View Progress Reports button.

Types of In Progress Reports

There are four progress reports.

Report	Description	Use
Critical Tasks	Shows a pie chart and table of all tasks on the critical path. Tasks on the critical path have no room for schedule slippage.	To see the status of all tasks on the critical path.
Late Tasks	Shows a pie chart and table of all tasks that are behind schedule.	To see which tasks are behind schedule.
Milestone Report	Shows three charts and tables about project milestones. The **Late Milestone** table shows milestones that are past due. The **Milestones Up Next** table shows milestones that are due in the next 30 days. The **Completed Milestones** table shows milestones that are 100% complete.	To see the status of all milestones.
Slipping Tasks	Shows a line chart and table of all tasks that are behind schedule.	To see tasks that have been or will be

Report	Description	Use
		completed later than planned.

> Access the Checklist tile on your LogicalCHOICE course screen for reference information and job aids on How to Use Existing Reports

ACTIVITY 4–1
Using Existing Reports

Data Files

C:\091111Data\Producing Project Reports\Residential Construction 4.mpp

Before You Begin

Microsoft Project Professional 2013 is open.

Scenario

The GreeneCentre residential construction project is nearing completion. Your project sponsor, Sylvia Deaton, has asked you to generate several status reports.

---

1. Open **C:\091111Data\Producing Project Reports\Residential Construction 4.mpp**.

2. Select the **REPORT** tab on the ribbon.

3. Generate a dashboard report.
   a) Select the **View Dashboard Reports** button.
   b) From the **View Dashboard Reports** drop-down list, select the **Project Overview** report.
      Notice the project completion percentage. Notice which top-level tasks are complete, in progress, and not yet started. Notice that there is a late task.

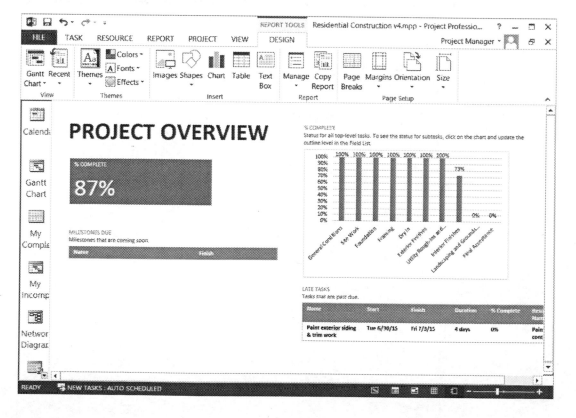

4. Generate a resources report.

a) If necessary, select the **REPORT** tab on the ribbon again.

b) Select the **View Resource Reports** button.

c) From the **View Resource Reports** drop-down list, select the **Resource Overview** report. Notice which resources have remaining work.

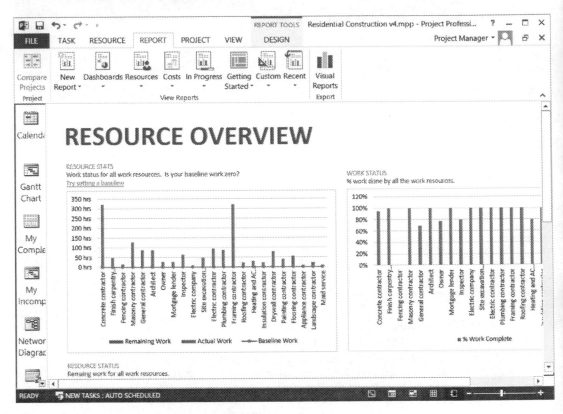

5. Generate a progress report.

a) If necessary, select the **REPORT** tab on the ribbon again.

b) Select the **View In Progress Reports** button.

c) From the **View In Progress Reports** drop-down list, select the **Critical Tasks** report. Notice the list of tasks on the critical path that are not complete.

6. Save the file in C:\091111Data\Producing Project Reports as *My Residential Construction 4.mpp* and then close the file.

TOPIC B

Create Custom Reports

You may find that Project 2013's built-in reports don't meet the needs of your project. In this topic, you will generate and customize new reports that fit your needs.

New Reports

You can start creating a new report by selecting the **New Report** button. Selecting this button will display four report options.

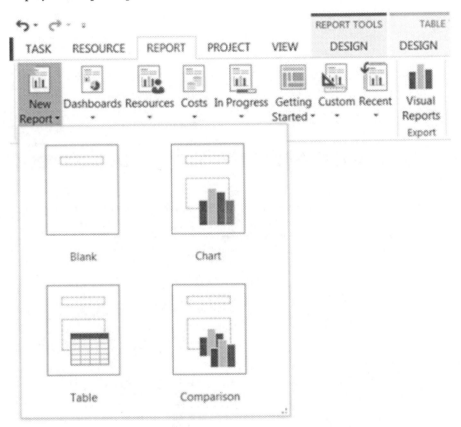

Figure 4–5: New Report button.

New Report Types

There are four types of new reports available.

Report	Description	Use
Blank Report	Generates a report that is empty except for the report title.	To create a report from scratch.
Chart	Generates a report that contains a report title and a single chart.	To show project information graphically.
Table	Generates a report that contains a report title and a single table.	To show project information in a tabular format.

Report	Description	Use
Comparison	Generates a report that contains a report title and two side-by-side charts.	To graphically compare two sets of project information.

You can customize each of these new report formats to meet your needs.

Report Design Commands

Whenever you generate a new report, the **REPORT TOOLS** contextual tab will appear on the ribbon. You can use the commands on this tab to change the overall look of the report.

Figure 4–6: Report design tools.

Here is a table of the commands on this tab and what they do.

Command	Description
Themes	Changes the graphic theme for the report. You can choose from over 20 themes.
Colors	Changes the color palette of the report. You can choose from over 20 color palettes, or create a custom palette.
Fonts	Changes the font combinations used in the report. You can choose from over 20 font combinations, or create your own.
Effects	Applies 3D effects to objects in the report.
Images	Inserts photos or graphics (such as your company logo) into the report.
Shapes	Inserts geometric shapes into the report.
Chart	Inserts a chart into the report.
Table	Inserts a table into the report.
Text Box	Inserts a text box into the report.
Manage	Enables you to rename the report. Also allows you to organize reports. Selecting the **Organizer** option will open the **Organizer** dialog box to the **Reports** tab. The **Reports** tab works exactly like the **Views** tab you learned about earlier in this course.
Copy Report	Copies the report to your Windows® clipboard so that you can paste it into another document.
Page Breaks	Allows you to see where the report will break when it is printed.
Margins	Allows you to set the margins for the printed report.
Orientation	Allows you to print the report in either **Portrait** or **Landscape** mode.
Size	Allows you to specify a page size for the printed report.

Chart Types

There are eight types of charts you can insert into a report, as well as several variations of each type from which to choose.

Chart Type	Example
Column	

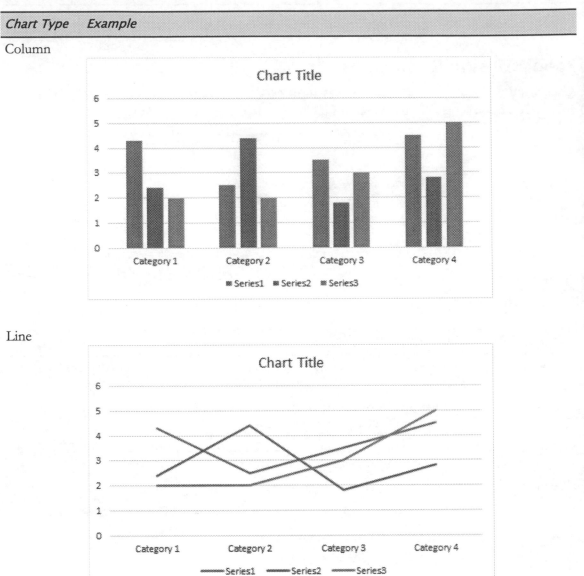

Line

Pie

Chart Type	Example

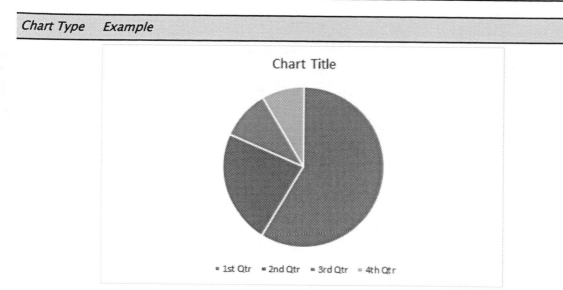

Bar

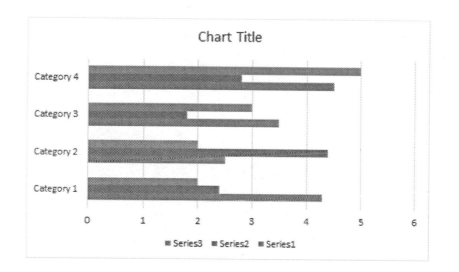

Area

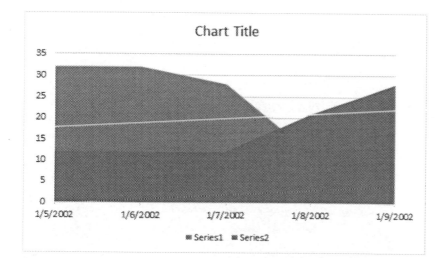

Surface

Chart Type	Example
	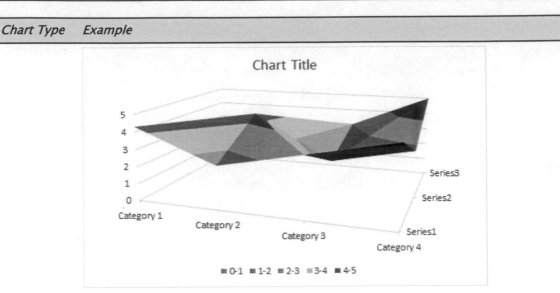
Radar	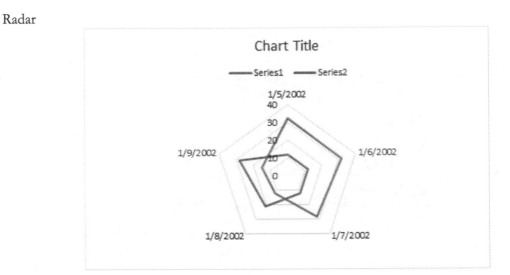
Combo	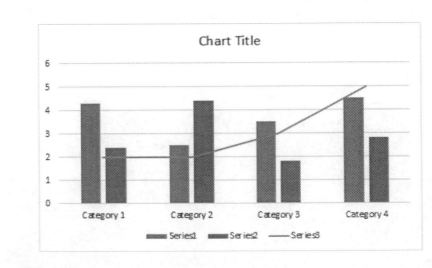

Chart Design Commands

If you generate a new chart report, a **CHART TOOLS DESIGN** contextual tab will appear on the ribbon. You can use the commands on this tab to change the look of the chart in the report.

Figure 4-7: Chart design tools.

Here is a table of the commands on this tab and what they do.

Command	Description
Add Chart Element	Adds titles, labels, and other elements to the chart.
Quick Layout	Changes how information is presented in the chart.
Change Colors	Changes the color scheme for the data elements (bars, lines, etc.) in the chart.
Chart Styles	Changes the graphical look of the chart.
Chart Data	Makes the **Field List** appear and disappear on the right side of the screen.
Change Chart Type	Changes the chart type (for example, from column chart to line chart).

 Note: You will learn how to use the **Field List** later in this topic.

Chart Format Commands

If you generate a new chart report, a **CHART TOOLS FORMAT** contextual tab will appear on the ribbon. You can use the commands on this tab to format any shapes or text boxes in the chart report.

Figure 4-8: Chart format tools.

 Note: These commands are very similar to the **DRAWING TOOLS FORMAT** contextual tab commands found in Word, Excel®, and PowerPoint®.

Table Design Commands

If you generate a new table report, a **TABLE TOOLS DESIGN** contextual tab will appear on the ribbon. You can use the commands on this tab to change the look of the table in the report.

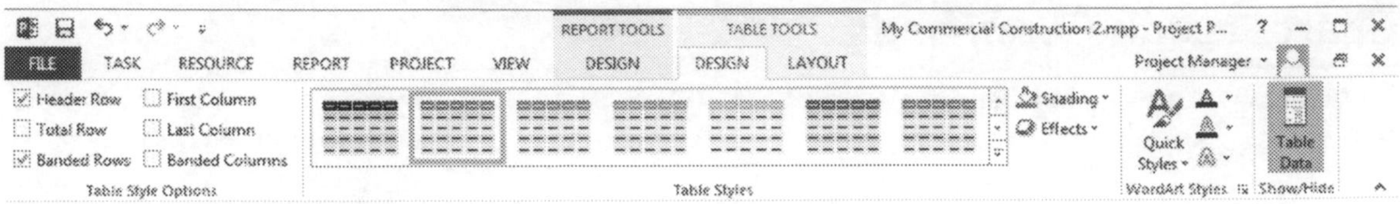

Figure 4-9: Table design tools.

Here is a table of the commands on this tab and what they do.

Command	Description
Table Style Options	Adds rows and columns to the table.
Table Styles	Changes the graphical look of the table.
Shading	Changes the shading of cells in the table.
Effects	Adds a shadow or reflection effects to the table.
WordArt Styles	Applies and formats WordArt in the table.
Table Data	Makes the **Field List** appear and disappear on the right side of the screen.

Table Layout Commands

If you generate a new table report, a **TABLE TOOLS LAYOUT** contextual tab will appear on the ribbon. You can use the commands on this tab to change the layout of the table in the report.

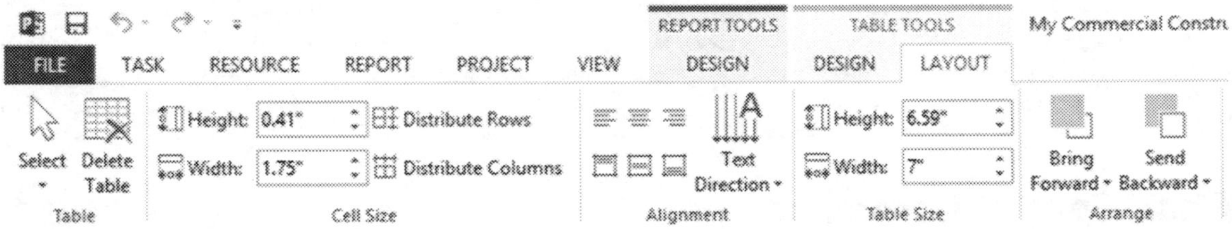

Figure 4-10: Table layout tools.

Here is a table of the commands on this tab and what they do.

Command	Description
Select	Selects the entire table, a column, or a row for layout.
Delete	Removes the table from the report.
Height (in the **Cell Size** command group)	Changes the height of the selected rows.
Width (in the **Cell Size** command group)	Changes the width of the selected columns.
Distribute Rows	Makes all selected rows the same height.
Distribute Columns	Makes all selected columns the same width.
Align Left	Aligns text in the selection to the left.
Center	Aligns text in the selection to the horizontal center.
Align Right	Aligns text in the selection to the right.
Align Top	Aligns text in the selection to the top.

Command	Description
Center Vertically	Aligns text in the selection to the vertical center.
Align Bottom	Aligns text in the selection to the bottom.
Text Direction	Changes the direction of text in the selection.
Height (in the **Table Size** command group)	Changes the height of the entire table.
Width (in the **Table Size** command group)	Changes the width of the entire table.
Bring Forward	If objects in the report overlap, brings the selected table forward or to the front.
Send Backward	If objects in the report overlap, sends the selected table backward or to the back.

The Field List

The **Field List** enables you to change which types of fields are displayed in the selected chart or table of a report. If a chart or table shows task information, selecting the **RESOURCES** tab in the **Field List** will cause resource information to be displayed in the chart (and vice versa).

Field List   ▾ ×

TASKS | **RESOURCES**

Select Category

| Name   ▾ |

Select Fields

☐ BCWS
☐ Budget Cost
☐ Cost
☐ Cost Per Use
☑ Cost Variance
☐ CV
☐ Overtime Cost
☐ Remaining Cost
☐ Remaining Overtime C
☐ SV
☐ VAC
▷ Duration
▷ Number

Cost Variance

Filter	All Resources ▾
Group By	No Group ▾
Outline Level	All Subtasks ▾
	☐ Show Hierarchy
Sort By	No Sort ▾

Figure 4-11: Field List pane.

Note: Earlier in this topic, you learned about using the **Chart Data** and **Table Data** buttons to make the **Field List** appear and disappear on the right side of the screen. The **Chart Data** and **Table Data** buttons are identical except for their names. If the **Chart Data** or **Table Data** button is toggled on, the **Field List** will appear automatically whenever you select a chart or table in a report. (This is true for new reports or built-in reports.)

Field List Options

The **Field List** includes many options for customizing charts and tables.

Area of Field List	Use
TASKS | **RESOURCES**	Choose to display task or resource information in the chart or table.
Select Category	Choose which type of data to display in the chart or table.
Select Fields	Choose which fields to display in the chart or table. For example, you might want to display cumulative cost or work fields.
Filter	Choose a criterion for displaying task or resource information in the chart or table. For example, you can use this field to specify a date range for information.
Group By	Choose a criterion for grouping task or resource information in the chart or table.
Outline Level	Choose the level of task information to be displayed in the chart or table. (Not active when displaying resource information.)
Sort By	Choose a criterion for sorting task or resource information in the chart or table.

Note: To further explore how customize Project 2013 reports, you can access the LearnTO **Customize Reports** presentation from the **LearnTO** tile on the LogicalCHOICE Course screen.

Edit Charts Quickly

Whenever you select a chart in a report, three buttons will pop up to the right of the chart. These buttons enable you to quickly edit the chart without using the ribbon or the **Field List.** When you select a button, Project 2013 will display several editing options.

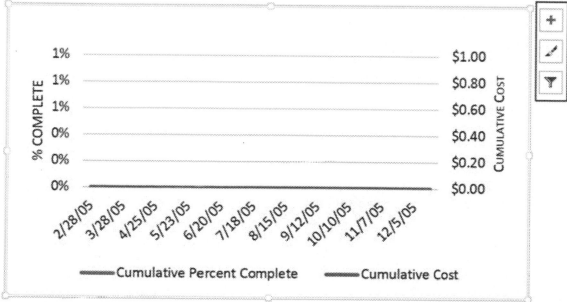

PROGRESS VERSUS COST

Progress made versus the cost spent over time. If % Complete line below the cumulative cost line, your project may be over budget.

Figure 4-12: Chart editing buttons.

This table describes the use of each button.

Button	Use
Chart Elements +	Use this button to add, subtract, or change chart elements such as the axes, axis title, chart title, data labels, data table, error bars, guidelines, legend, trendline, and up/down bars.
Chart Styles	Use this button to change the style and color of the chart.
Chart Filters ▼	Use this button to change the data series and categories displayed on the chart.

Hyperlinks in Reports

There may be circumstances when you need to refer to additional data in your report. This data may be inside or outside of the Project file. Say, for example, that you are creating a report on a Six Sigma project in your organization. Since some of your readers may not be familiar with Six Sigma, you want to point them to a website URL with supplemental information about Six Sigma. You can easily do this by adding a text box to the report and adding a hyperlink to the text box.

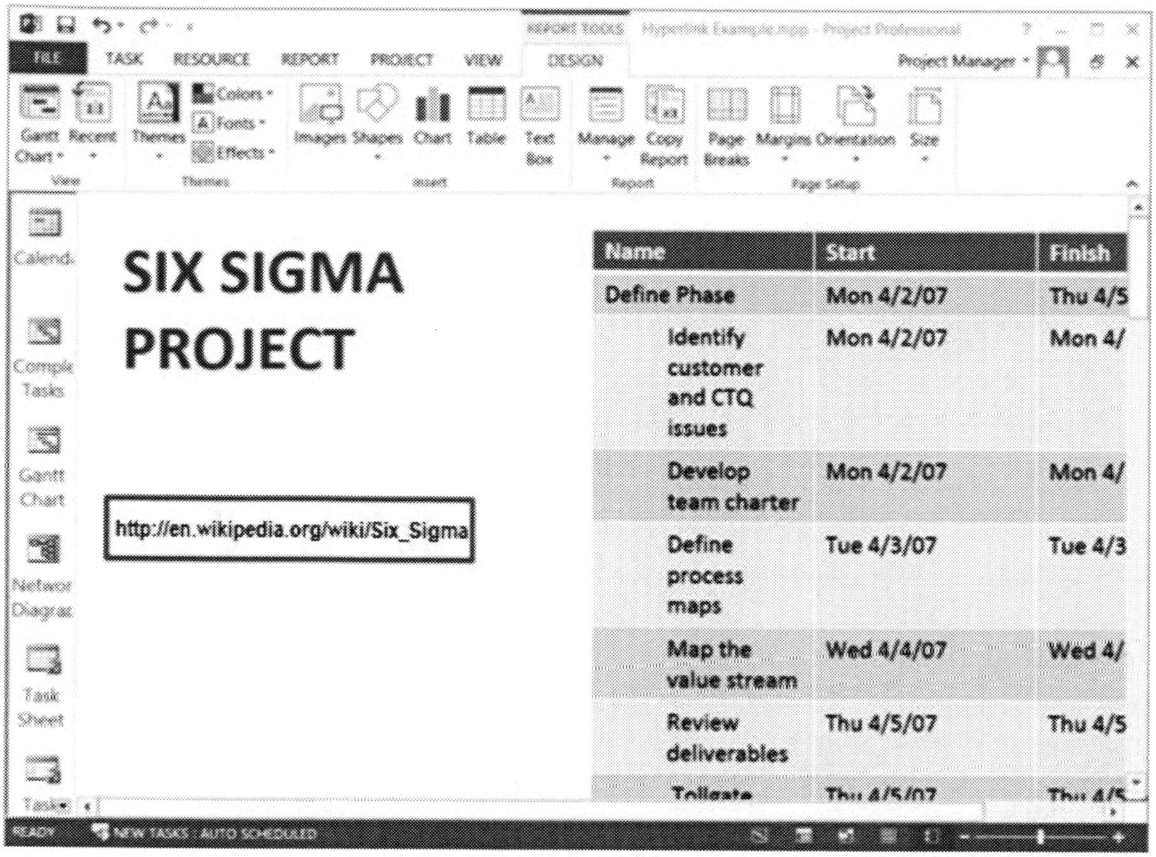

Figure 4-13: Hyperlink-enabled text box in a report.

You can add the text box to the report by selecting the **Draw a Text Box** button on the **REPORT TOOLS DESIGN** contextual tab. You can add a hyperlink to the text box by right-clicking on the text box and selecting the **Hyperlink** option from the menu.

When you select the **Hyperlink** option from the menu, Project 2013 will display an **Insert Hyperlink** dialog box.

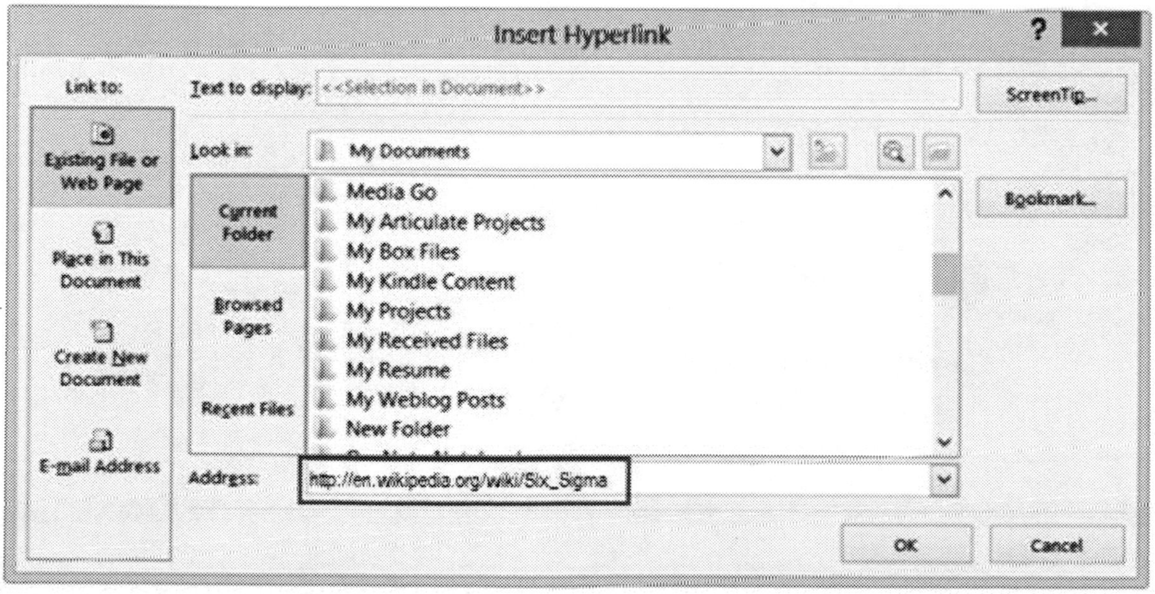

Figure 4-14: Hyperlink dialog box.

This dialog box gives you several options for creating hyperlinks. You can link to:

- Existing files (Microsoft Word, Excel, PowerPoint, Project, and more) or web pages. This includes bookmarks in existing files.
- Another view or report in the same Project 2013 file.
- A new file (Microsoft Word, Excel, PowerPoint, Project, and more).
- An email address.

> **Note:** In most programs, unvisited hyperlinked text is shown as underlined and blue font. This is not the case for hyperlinked text boxes in Project 2013. This is because the hyperlink is applied to the text box as a whole, rather than the text within the text box.

> **Note:** It's a good idea to type the URL itself into the text box, as well as in the **Hyperlink** dialog box. That way, it you export the report to PDF, Adobe Acrobat Reader will recognize and enable the text as a hyperlink.

> **Note:** You can also add hyperlinks to images and shapes that you insert into Project reports.

Images in Reports

Adding an image to report can make it more interesting and informative. You can also add an image to "brand" the report with the your organization or project logo.

Let's continue our earlier example of a report on a Six Sigma project in your organization. You realize that some of your readers are not familiar with the DMAIC cycle used in the project, so you decide to add an image to the report that illustrates the process.

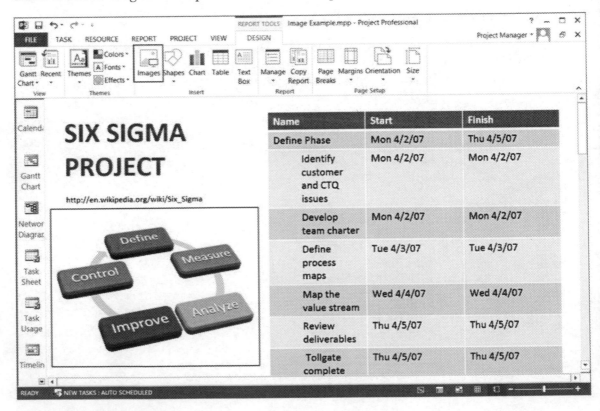

Figure 4–15: Image added to report.

You can add an image to the report by selecting the **Images (From File)** button on the **REPORT TOOLS DESIGN** contextual tab. When you select this button, an **Insert Image** dialog box will open so that you can navigate to the location of the desired image and choose it.

> **Access the Checklist tile on your LogicalCHOICE course screen for reference information and job aids on How to Create a Custom Report**

ACTIVITY 4-2
Creating Custom Reports

Data Files

C:\091111Data\Producing Project Reports\Commercial Construction 4.mpp

C:\091111Data\Producing Project Reports\GreeneCentre Logo.png

Before You Begin

Microsoft Project Professional 2013 is open.

Scenario

The GreeneCentre commercial construction project has been in progress for a year now. Your project sponsor, Sylvia Deaton, asks you to generate a new custom report for the board of directors with the following elements:

- A table of high-level tasks (or phases) that have been completed.
- A chart of remaining work.
- A link to the GreeneCentre website.
- The GreeneCentre logo.

---

1. Open C:\091111Data\Producing Project Reports\Commercial Construction 4.mpp.

2. Select the **REPORT** tab on the ribbon.

3. Create a new table report.
   a) Select the **New Report** button.

   New
   Report ▾

   b) From the **New Report** drop-down list, select the **Table** option.

   Table

   c) In the **Report Name** dialog box, in the **Name** field, type *GreeneCentre Commercial Construction*
   d) Select **OK** to close the dialog box.
   Notice that a new table report appears. Notice, too, that the **TABLE TOOLS** contextual tab and the **Field List** are now visible so that you can modify the table.

4. Design the table.
   a) Make sure the table in the report is selected. If it is not, select it.
   b) On the **TABLE TOOLS DESIGN** contextual tab, in the **Table Style** command group, select **Medium Style 2 - Accent 6**.
      Notice the table now has a green style.

5. Use the **Field List**.
   a) Make sure the table in the report is selected. If it is not, select it.
   b) At the top of the **Field List**, make sure **TASKS** is selected. If it is not, select it.
   c) In the **Filter** field, select **Completed Tasks** from the drop-down list.
   d) In the **Outline Level** field, select **Level 1** from the drop-down list.
   e) Select the **Close** button in the upper-right corner of the **Field List** to close it.
      Notice that the table now contains information about high-level completed tasks.

Name	Start	Finish	% Complete
Long Lead Procurement	Wed 1/7/15	Tue 4/14/15	100%
Mobilize on Site	Tue 1/6/15	Mon 1/19/15	100%
Site Grading and Utilities	Tue 1/20/15	Mon 3/9/15	100%
Foundations	Tue 3/10/15	Thu 4/23/15	100%
Steel Erection	Fri 4/24/15	Thu 6/25/15	100%

6. Add a chart to the report.
   a) Scroll down the report until the table is no longer visible on the screen.
   b) In the **REPORT TOOLS DESIGN** contextual tab, find the **Insert** command group and select the **Add a Chart** button.

   Chart

   c) In the **Insert Chart** dialog box, find and select the **Clustered Column** option and select **OK**.

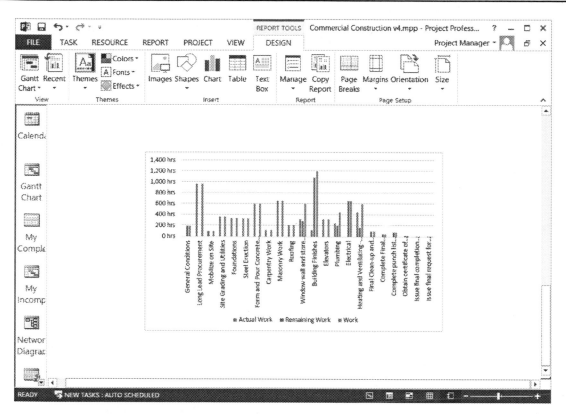

7. Use the chart edit buttons.

   a) Select the chart to display the chart edit buttons.

   b) Select the **Chart Elements** button. ⊹

   c) In the **CHART ELEMENTS** pop-up box, uncheck **Gridlines**.
      Notice that the gridlines are no longer visible on the chart.

   d) If necessary, select the chart to display the chart edit buttons again.

   e) Select the **Chart Styles** button. ✐

   f) From the **Chart Styles** pop-up box, select the **COLOR** tab.

   g) Scroll down the **Color 10** option (which is different shades of green) and select it.

   h) If necessary, select the chart to display the chart edit buttons again.
      Notice that the bars on the chart are now different shades of green.

   i) Select the **Chart Filters** button. ▼

   j) In the **Chart Filters** pop-up box, in the **Series** section, uncheck **Actual Work** and **Work**, leaving only
      Remaining Work checked. Select the **Apply** button.
      Notice that only the **Remaining Work** series is displayed on the chart.

8. Insert a hyperlinked text box.

   a) Scroll up to the top of the report.

   b) Select the **REPORT TOOLS DESIGN** contextual tab on the ribbon, find the **Insert** command group, and select the **Draw a Text Box** button.

   c) Move the mouse pointer to the white space below the report title and draw a text box.

d) Type *http://www.greenecentre.example* in the text field.

e) Right-click and select the Hyperlink option.
f) In the Insert Hyperlink dialog box, make sure the Existing File or Web Page option is selected and type *http://www.greenecentre.example* into the Address field.
g) Select OK to close the Insert Hyperlink dialog box.

9. Insert an image.
   a) Select the REPORT TOOLS DESIGN contextual tab on the ribbon, find the Insert command group, and select the Images (From File) button.
   b) Navigate to C:\091111Data\Producing Project Reports, select GreeneCentre Logo.png, and select the Insert button.

c) Move and resize the logo until it covers GreeneCentre in the report title.

10. Save the file in C:\091111Data\Producing Project Reports as *My Commercial Construction 4.mpp*

TOPIC C

Export Visual Reports

If you use Microsoft Excel or Microsoft Visio® extensively, you will be glad to know that you can export your project data from Project to Excel and Visio. In this topic, you will export project information using visual reports.

Visual Reports

Visual Reports enable you to export your project's data to a PivotChart in Microsoft Excel and to a PivotDiagram in Microsoft Visio. These views provide a way for you to choose what fields, including custom fields, to display in a report while viewing it, and quickly modify how the report is displayed without having to regenerate it from within Project 2013. With this flexibility, Visual Reports provide a more agile reporting solution than basic reports.

Figure 4–16: Visual Reports button.

Excel PivotCharts

In Excel, a PivotChart report can help you visualize Project 2013 data so that you can easily see comparisons, patterns, and trends. This will enable you to make informed decisions about critical data in your project.

Visio PivotDiagrams

In Microsoft Visio, a PivotDiagram is a collection of shapes arranged in a tree structure that helps you to analyze and summarize data in a visual, easy-to-understand format. It starts out as a single shape, called a top node, that contains information imported from Project 2013. You can break the top node into a level of subnodes to view your data in various ways.

Visual Reports Dialog Box Options

When you select the **Visual Reports** button, the **Visual Reports - Create Report** dialog box will be displayed. In this dialog box, you can choose which built-in Excel or Visio templates you want to use and what timescale you want to include in the report. The Visual Report generated by the dialog box will automatically open as a new Excel or Visio file. You can modify the Visual Report in Excel or Visio and save it in those file formats.

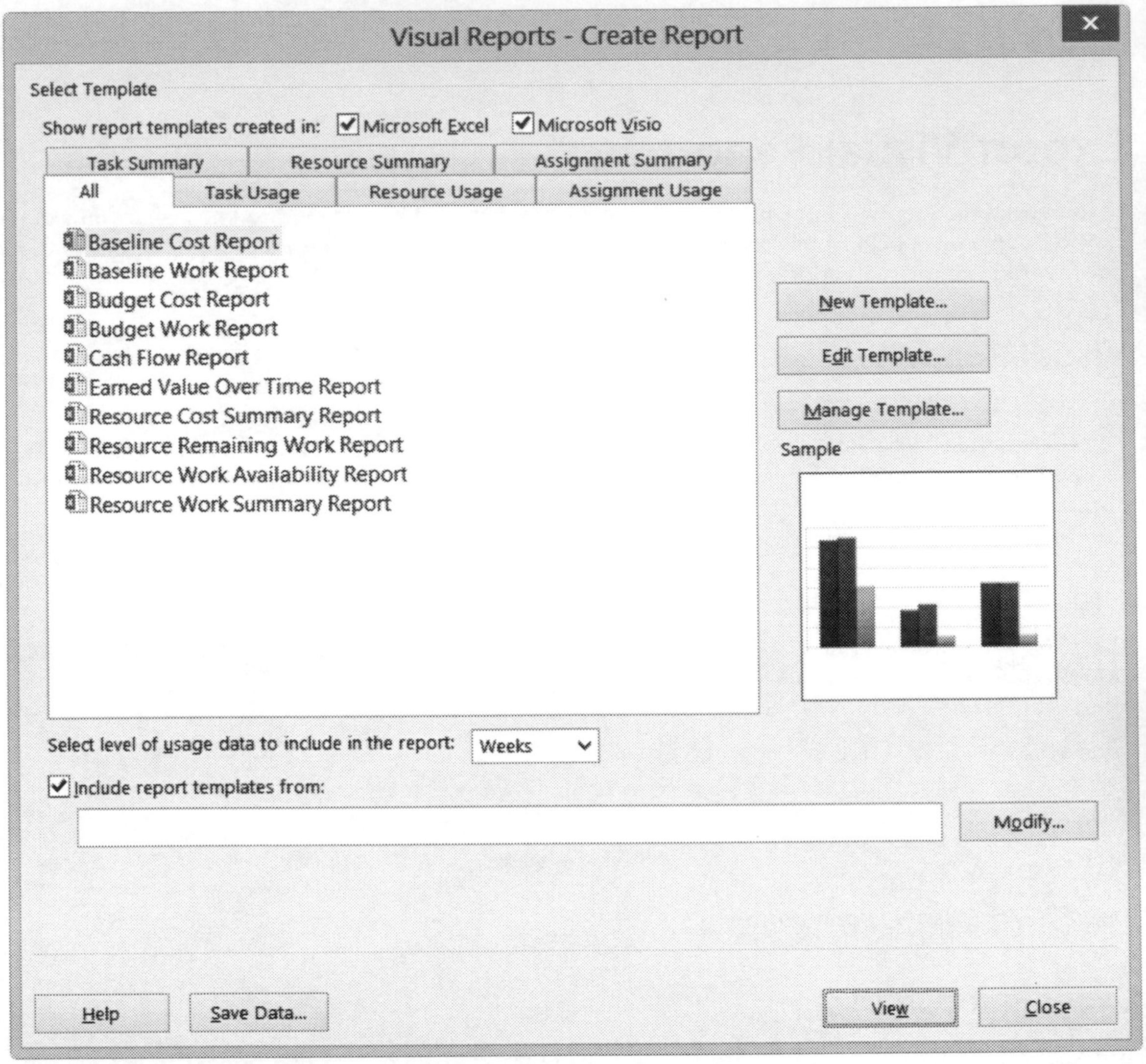

Figure 4-17: Visual Reports – Create Report dialog box.

Note: You can only create Visual Reports for applications that are installed on your computer. If you do not have Excel or Visio, you will not see those templates in the **Visual Reports - Create Report** dialog box.

Note: You can do much with Visual Reports from this dialog box. However, given the complexity of the procedures and the limited number of students who are likely to use them, they are not covered in this course.

Access the Checklist tile on your LogicalCHOICE course screen for reference information and job aids on How to Export a Visual Report

ACTIVITY 4–3
Exporting Visual Reports

Before You Begin
My Commercial Construction 4.mpp is open.

Scenario
Your project sponsor, Sylvia Deaton, asks you to generate a Baseline Work Report for the GreeneCentre commercial construction project that she can manipulate in Excel.

---

1. Open the **Visual Reports - Create Report** dialog box.
   a) Select the **REPORT** tab on the ribbon.
   b) Find the **Export** command group.
   c) Select the **Visual Reports** button.

   Visual
   Reports

   The **Visual Reports - Create Report** dialog box will open.

2. Set the parameters for the Visual Report.

a) In the **Visual Reports - Create Report** dialog box, select the **All** tab.

b) On the **All** tab, select the **Baseline Work Report** with an Excel icon next to it.

Baseline Work Report

c) In the **Select level of usage data to include in the report** field, select **Days** from the drop-down list.

d) Select **View**.

e) Wait for Project 2013 to generate an Excel PivotChart. This can take several seconds.
Notice that Excel 2013 opens automatically and displays a PivotChart.

3. Save the created Excel file in C:\091111Data\Producing Project Reports as *My Baseline Work Report.xlsx* and close the file.

4. Close My Commercial Construction 4.mpp.

Summary

In this lesson, you learned how to produce project reports.

Which of Project 2013's built-in reports do you find most useful, and why?

What kind of custom report are you most likely to build, and why?

> **Note:** If your instructor/organization is incorporating social media resources as part of this training, use the LogicalCHOICE Course screen to search for or begin conversations regarding this lesson.

Course Follow-Up

Congratulations! You have completed the *Microsoft® Project 2013: Part 2* course. You are now able to use many of the advanced features and functions of Microsoft Project Professional 2013 so that you can use it effectively and efficiently in a real-world environment.

The ability to complete projects on time, within budget, and according to specifications is crucial for all professionals—regardless of whether project management is an official part of your duties. Microsoft Project Professional 2013 is a powerful tool that can enable you to manage projects effectively and efficiently.

What's Next?

Spend as much time as you can, as soon as you can, using Project 2013 to create and manage actual project plans. The more real-world experience you have with the program, the more proficient you will become.

Since Project 2013 has many features in common with other Office programs, also consider taking additional Office 2013 course offerings from Logical Operations.

You are encouraged to explore Project further by actively participating in any of the social media forums set up by your instructor or training administrator through the **Social Media** tile on the LogicalCHOICE Course screen.

A | Managing Projects with Microsoft Project 2013 Exam 74–343

Selected Logical Operations courseware addresses Microsoft Specialist certification skills for Managing Projects with Microsoft Project 2013. The following table indicates where Project 2013 skills that are tested on Exam 74-343 are covered in the Logical Operations Microsoft Project 2013 series of courses.

Objective Domain	Covered In
1. Initialize a Project	
1.1 Create a new project	
1.1.1 Creating a template from a completed project	Part 1
1.1.2 Creating a project from an existing template, existing project, SharePoint task list, or Microsoft Office Excel workbook	Part 1
1.2 Create and maintain calendars	
1.2.1 Setting working or non-working hours and days for calendars	Part 1
1.2.2 Setting a base calendar, resource calendar, and hours per day	Part 1
1.2.3 Applying calendars to project, task, and resource levels	Part 1
1.3 Create custom fields	
1.3.1 Creating basic formulas, graphical indicator criteria, lookup tables, and task and resource custom fields	Part 2, Topic 1-C
1.4 Customize option settings	
1.4.1 Setting default task types, manual vs. auto-scheduling, project options, calendar options, customized ribbon and quick access toolbar	Part 2, Topic 1-D; Part 1
2. Create a Task-Based Schedule	
2.1 Set up project information	
2.1.1 Defining project start date	Part 1
2.1.2 Applying calendars and current date	Part 1
2.1.3 Entering project properties	Part 1

Objective Domain	Covered In
2.1.4 Displaying the project summary task on a new project	Part 1
2.2 Create and modify a project task structure	
2.2.1 Creating and modifying summary tasks and subtasks	Part 1
2.2.2 Rearranging tasks	Part 2, Topic 2-A
2.2.3 Creating milestones	Part 1
2.2.4 Creating manually scheduled tasks	Part 1
2.2.5 Outlining	Part 1
2.2.6 Setting tasks as active or inactive	Part 1
2.3 Build a logical schedule model	
2.3.1 Setting date constraints, deadlines, dependencies, links, duration equations, effort-driven tasks, and formulas	Part 2, Topic 1-C; Part 1
2.3.2 Choosing a task type	Part 1, Topic 3-A
2.4 Create a user-controlled schedule	
2.4.1 Entering duration	Part 1
2.4.2 Setting or changing the task mode (manual or auto)	Part 1
2.4.3 Displaying warnings and suggestions	Part 1
2.4.4 Using estimated durations and user-controlled summary tasks	Part 1
2.5 Manage multiple projects	
2.5.1 Creating a shared resource pool	Part 1
2.5.2 Connecting to a resource pool	Part 1
2.5.3 Creating links between projects	Part 2, Topic 1-A
2.5.4 Resolving conflicts between linked projects	Part 2, Topic 1-A
2.5.5 Working with master projects and sub-projects	Part 2, Topic 1-A
2.5.6 Summarizing data in master projects	Part 2, Topic 1-A
3. Manage Resources and Assignments	
3.1 Enter and edit resource information	
3.1.1 Entering and editing max units resource types resource rate table cost per use availability resource group generic resources and cost resources	Part 1
3.2 Create and edit resource assignments	
3.2.1 Using task forms	Part 2, Topic 3-B
3.2.2 Assigning multiple resources	Part 1
3.2.3 Assigning resources to tasks using units that represent part-time work	Part 1
3.2.4 Editing assignments	Part 1
3.3 Manage resource allocation	
3.3.1 Viewing task and resource usage	Part 1

Objective Domain	Covered In
3.3.2 Viewing availability across multiple projects	Part 2, Topic 1-A
3.3.3 Changing assignment information	Part 1
3.3.4 Leveling	Part 1
3.3.5 Replacing resources	Part 1
3.4 Manage resource allocations by using Team Planner	
3.4.1 Displaying current resource allocations and assignments	Part 1
3.4.2 Managing unassigned tasks	Part 1
3.4.3 Resolving resource conflicts	Part 1
3.4.4 Leveling resource overallocations	Part 1
3.4.5 Substituting resources	Part 1
3.5 Model project costs	
3.5.1 Entering and assigning resource-based costs (work material cost) cost per use fixed costs accrual method	Part 1
3.5.2 Applying a resource rate table	Part 1
4. Track and Analyze a Project	
4.1 Set and maintain baselines	
4.1.1 Using multiple baselines	Part 2, Topic 1-B; LearnTO Baseline a Project
4.1.2 Baselining an entire project	Part 2, Topic 1-B
4.1.3 Baselining selected tasks	Part 2, Topic 1-B
4.1.4 Updating a baseline	Part 2, Topic 1-B; LearnTO Baseline a Project
4.2 Update actual progress	
4.2.1 Updating percentage completion, actual or remaining duration, actual work, remaining work, status date, current date, actual start and actual finish	Part 2, Topic 2-E
4.2.2 Using actual work and usage views	Part 2, Topic 3-B
4.2.3 Rescheduling uncompleted work	Part 2, Topic 2-E
4.2.4 Cancelling an unneeded task	Part 1
4.3 Compare progress against a baseline	
4.3.1 Using date variance, work variance, cost variance, and task slippage	Part 2, Topic 1-B
4.3.2 Showing variance of the current plan against baseline (tracking Gantt)	Part 2, Topic 3-B
4.3.3 Selecting a view to display variance	Part 2, Topic 1-B
4.4 Resolve potential schedule problems	
4.4.1 Displaying warnings suggestions and task drivers by using Task Inspector and Task Path	Part 2, Topic 2-A

Objective Domain	Covered In
4.4.2 Identifying resource overallocations	Part 1
4.5 Display Critical Path information	
4.5.3 Viewing the critical path in single or master projects	Part 2, Topic 2-C
4.5.4 Viewing total slack	Part 2, Topic 2-D
4.5.5 Displaying progress against baseline or deadlines	Part 2, Topic 1-B
5. Communicate Project Information	
5.1 Apply and customize views	
5.1.1 Using auto-filter	Part 2, Topic 3-A
5.1.2 Applying views	Part 2, Topic 3-B; Part 1
5.1.3 Grouping	Part 2, Topic 3-A
5.1.4 Filtering	Part 2, Topic 3-A
5.1.5 Highlighting	Part 2, Topic 3-A
5.1.6 Creating and managing tables	Part 2, Topic 3-A
5.1.7 Sorting	Part 2, Topic 3-A
5.1.8 Customizing views	Part 2, Topic 3-C; LearnTO Customize Views
5.1.9 Importing data from Excel	Part 1
5.2 Share data with other applications	
5.2.1 Exporting data to Excel	Part 1
5.2.2 Attaching documents or linking hyperlinks to supporting information	Part 2, Topic 3-A; Part 1
5.2.3 Copying and pasting timeline and reports to other Office Web Apps	Part 2, Topics 3-D, 4-B
5.2.4 Creating and generating visual reports in Excel and Microsoft Visio	Part 2, Topic 4-C
5.2.5 Exporting a timeline view to e-mail	Part 2, Topic 3-D
5.3 Configure and display reports and dashboards	
5.3.1 Reporting progress status	Part 2, Topic 4-A
5.3.2 Saving to PDF or XPS	Part 1
5.3.3 Displaying Gantt information, schedule, or timeline	Part 2, Topics 3-B, 3-D; Part 1
5.3.4 Displaying data based on date range	Part 2, Topic 4-B
5.3.5 Creating built-in dashboards and reports	Part 2, Topic 4-A
5.3.6 Changing and customizing built-in dashboards and reports	Part 2, Topics 4-B, 4-C; LearnTO Customize Reports
5.3.7 Copying pictures	Part 2, Topic 4-B
5.3.8 Working with cumulative fields	Part 2, Topic 4-B
5.4 Connect and share data with SharePoint	

Objective Domain	Covered In
5.4.1 Syncing to SharePoint	Part 1
5.4.2 Sharing plans and getting updates through SharePoint	Part 1
5.4.3 Sharing project plans through SharePoint (bi-directional sync of tasks progress and timeline elements)	Part 1
5.4.4 Collecting actual progress from a team through SharePoint	Part 1
5.5 Extend Project 2013	
5.5.1 Acquiring Apps from the Office Store	Part 2, Topic 1-E
5.5.2 Saving files in SkyDrive	Part 1
5.5.3 Acquiring templates from office com	Part 1
5.5.5 Automating frequent tasks with visual basic for applications (VBA)	Part 2, Topic 1-E

Lesson Labs

Lesson labs are provided for certain lessons as additional learning resources for this course. Lesson labs are developed for selected lessons within a course in cases when they seem most instructionally useful as well as technically feasible. In general, labs are supplemental, optional unguided practice and may or may not be performed as part of the classroom activities. Your instructor will consider setup requirements, classroom timing, and instructional needs to determine which labs are appropriate for you to perform, and at what point during the class. If you do not perform the labs in class, your instructor can tell you if you can perform them independently as self-study, and if there are any special setup requirements.

Lesson Lab 1–1
Managing the Project Environment

Activity Time: 15 minutes.

Data Files

C:\091111Data\Managing the Project Environment\Market Research Schedule 1.mpp

C:\091111Data\Managing the Project Environment\New Business Plan 1.mpp

Before You Begin

Microsoft Project 2013 is open.

Scenario

You and an entrepreneurial friend believe you have a lucrative idea for a new mobile phone app. In preparation for launching your own start-up company, your friend creates a Project 2013 file for conducting market research and you create a Project 2013 file for writing a business plan. You and your friend are meeting together to merge the files, baseline the combined project, and add a custom field.

---

1. Create a new blank project file. Insert **Market Research Schedule 1.mpp** and **New Business Plan 1.mpp** into it as subprojects.

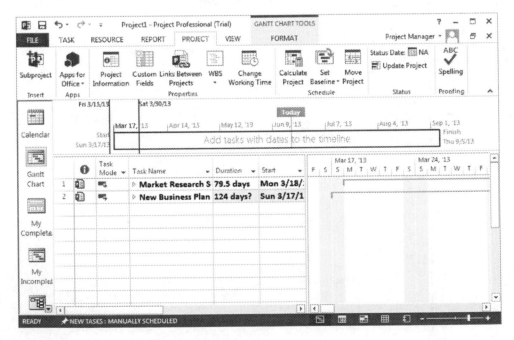

2. Set the initial baseline for the project.

3. Create a custom field by renaming the **Resource Text1** field to *Operating System*. Then, make the renamed field into a lookup table with four values (*A, B, G, M*) and four corresponding descriptions (*Apple iOS 7, Blackberry 10, Google Android 4, Microsoft Windows RT*).

4. Save the file in **C:\091111Data\Managing the Project Environment** as *My Awesome App Project Plan 1.mpp* and then close the file.

Lesson Lab 2–1
Managing Task Structures

Activity Time: 15 minutes

Data Files

C:\091111Data\Managing Task Structures\Awesome App Project Plan 2.mpp

Before You Begin

Microsoft Project 2013 is open.

Scenario

You and your business partner are implementing a project plan to conduct market research and write a business plan for a new mobile phone app. A couple of weeks into the plan, you realize that a few changes are needed to the task structure.

---

1. Open **Awesome App Project Plan 2.mpp**.

2. Expand the *Market Research Schedule* and *New Business Plan* summary tasks.

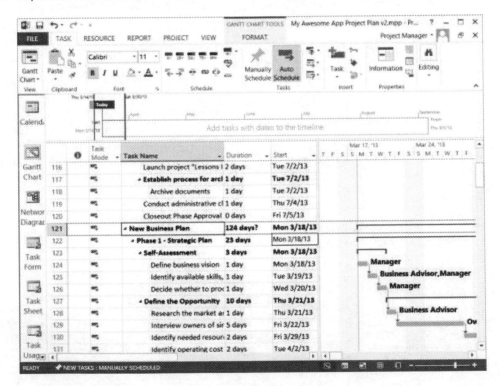

3. Change the task list.
   a) Delete the **Define the Market** summary task (row 148) and its subtasks because these tasks are covered by the **Market Research Schedule** tasks.

b) Link **Closeout Phase Approval** (row 120) and **Define business vision** (row 124).

4. Add lag and lead to project tasks.

a) Add 3 days of lag to the FS dependency between **Estimate the competition** (row 139) and **Assess market size and stability task** (row 140).

b) Add 3 days of lead to the FS dependency between **Review personal suitability** (row 143) and **Evaluate initial profitability** (row 144).

5. Save the file in C:\091111Data\Managing Task Structures as *My Awesome App Project Plan 2.mpp* and then close the file.

Lesson Lab 3-1
Generating Project Views

Activity Time: 15 minutes

Data Files

C:\091111Data\Generating Project Views\Awesome App Project Plan 3.mpp

Before You Begin

Microsoft Project 2013 is open.

Scenario

You and your business partner are monitoring and controlling a project plan to conduct market research and write a business plan for a new mobile phone app. You want to use Project 2013's **VIEW** tab to make this process more effective and efficient.

1. Open **Awesome App Project Plan 3.mpp**.

2. Use view commands.

   a) Use the **Outline** button to show all subtasks.

   b) Highlight the summary tasks.

c) Hide the **Timeline** view in the upper pane.

3. Create a custom view.
   a) Start a new combination view named *Task Relationships*

b) Make **Relationship Diagram** the **Primary View** and **Task Details Form** the **Details Pane**.

4. Save the file in **C:\091111Data\Generating Project Views** as *My Awesome App Project Plan 3.mpp* and then close the file.

Lesson Lab 4–1
Generating Project Reports

Activity Time: 15 minutes

Data Files
C:\091111Data\Producing Project Reports\Awesome App Project Plan 4.mpp

Before You Begin
Microsoft Project 2013 is open.

Scenario
You and your business partner are monitoring and controlling a project plan to conduct market research and write a business plan for a new mobile phone app. You want to create reports that will enable you to easily see the status of your project.

1. Open **Awesome App Project Plan 4.mpp.**

2. Use existing reports.
   a) Generate a **Project Overview** report using the **Dashboards** button.

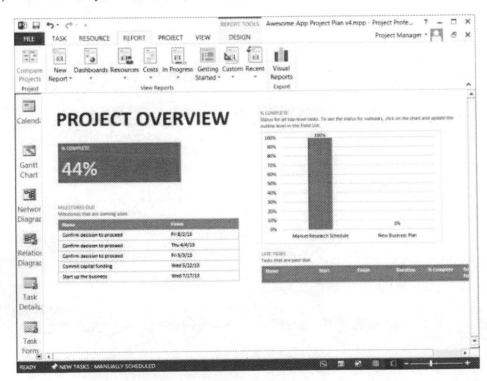

   b) Generate a **Milestone Report** using the **In Progress** button.

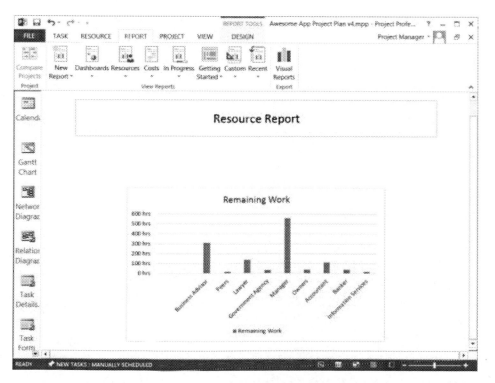

3. Create custom reports.

   a) Start a new report, using the **Chart** option, named *Resource Report*

   b) Use the **Field List** and chart editing buttons to show the **Remaining Work** of project resources on the chart.

   c) Start a new report, using the **Table** option, named *Task Report*

   d) Use the **Field List** to show **Incomplete Tasks** at **Outline Level 3** in the table.

4. Save the file in **C:\091111Data\Producing** Project Reports as *My Awesome App Project Plan 4.mpp* and then close the file.

Solutions

ACTIVITY 2–3: Managing the Critical Path

3. Which tasks above have zero total slack? (Select two.)

   ☑ Conduct finish plumbing inspection

   ☐ Complete 1st floor circuits to service panel

   ☐ Complete 2nd floor circuits to service panel

   ☑ Complete communications wiring - phone, cable, computer, alarm

   These two tasks have zero total slack because they are on the critical path.

5. True or False? If the task Finalize plans and develop estimate with owner, architect takes longer than 20 days to complete, the project will still finish on time.

   ☐ True

   ☑ False

   This task is on the critical path, so if the task does not finish on time, the project will not finish on time.

Glossary

FF

(Finish-to-Finish) A dependency between two tasks in which the first task must be completed before the second task can be completed.

FS

(Finish-to-Start) A dependency between two tasks in which the first task must be completed before the second task can begin.

SF

(Start-to-Finish) A dependency between two tasks in which the first task must begin before the second task can be completed.

baseline

A measurement, calculation, or location used as a basis for comparison.

critical path

The longest path in a project, calculated by summing the durations of the individual tasks in the path, that determines the duration of the project.

custom field

A data field that you can configure for your unique project or organizational needs.

dependency

A logical relationship between two tasks in which the start or finish of one task affects the start or finish of the other.

earned value

The budgeted cost of work performed as of a specific status date.

float (slack)

The amount of time that a task can be delayed without affecting its successors (free float) or the project completion date (total float).

lag

A delay in time between two tasks that are linked together.

lead

An overlap in time between two tasks that are linked together.

link

In Project 2013, the act or result of joining two tasks together to create a dependency.

master project

A project that is linked to one or more smaller subprojects.

network diagramming

A method for illustrating project information that emphasizes task sequencing and dependencies among tasks. Tasks are depicted as boxes (known as nodes), and dependencies are depicted as arrows connecting the nodes. Also known as Precedence Diagramming Method (PDM).

path
A chain of linked tasks from a starting point to an ending point.

predecessor
A task that must be started or finished before another task can be performed.

project baseline
An approved plan for a project.

project sponsor
The person in an organization who authorizes, supports, and approves a project.

project stakeholder
Anyone who is actively involved in a project or has an interest in its outcome.

rollup
Including lower-level project information at higher levels of the project.

SS
(Start-to-Start) A dependency between two tasks in which the first task must begin before the second task can begin.

subproject
A project that is linked to a larger master project.

successor
A task that is logically linked to one or more predecessor tasks.

summary task
A task that has related subtasks grouped below it.

variance
The difference between baseline and actual performance.

Index

091111S rev 2.0
ISBN-13 978-1-4246-2116-3
ISBN-10 1-4246-2116-X

9 781424 621163